Stelmark

A FAMILY RECOLLECTION

Warm regards,

Harry Mark Petrakis

Stelmark

A FAMILY RECOLLECTION

HARRY MARK PETRAKIS

DAVID McKAY COMPANY, INC.

NEW YORK

STELMARK: A FAMILY RECOLLECTION

COPYRIGHT © 1970 BY HARRY MARK PETRAKIS

Chapter IV was originally published as "Love Letter to an Era That's Past" in the *Chicago Sun-Times* in 1965. (Reprinted with permission from *Chicago Sun-Times* MIDWEST Magazine.)

Chapter V was originally published as "A Gift of Figs" in the quarterly *Chicago* in 1965.

Chapter VI was originally published as "Summers That Quickly Pass" in the *Chicago Tribune* in 1967.

LIBRARY OF CONGRESS CATALOG CARD NUMBER: 76-124685

MANUFACTURED IN THE UNITED STATES OF AMERICA

Typography by Janet Halverson

FOR MY BROTHER DAN, WHO HAS MET ADVERSITY
WITH A RARE FAITH AND COURAGE.

Sometimes it crosses my mind that the things I write here are nothing other than images that prisoners or sailors tattoo on their skin.

GEORGE SEFERIS

Stelmark

A FAMILY RECOLLECTION

Prologue

NOSTALGIA is something I have always known. Although I have never been to Crete, the island where my father and mother were born, the constellations of my childhood shimmered with stories of that tragic and lovely land. For many years I believed that when I finally made the journey to Crete for the first time, it would be a jubilant homecoming for a prodigal or an exile.

I am no longer sure when I make the journey of what I will find. The years have made me understand that we remain wanderers, in transit all our lives, seeking a haven that somehow remains just out of reach. Or is the answer simply that I have lost the faith of childhood?

Once I felt I belonged indelibly to that island where tall cypresses cast long shadows across the graves of my grandparents and great-grandparents. The songs, tales, ballads, and proverbs passed from my parents to me.

I knew the myths that were steeped in blood. On

11

that dark, mysterious island, Minos reigned; his wife was possessed of a demon-driven lust for a bull, and that union gave birth to the Minotaur that the king imprisoned in the labyrinth. Theseus came and killed the monster, fleeing to freedom following Ariadne's golden thread. From that island, Idomeneus, Prince of Crete, set sail for Troy to join the Greeks in avenging the flexuous Helen.

If the myths sometimes seemed spectral, the Cretans of my childhood abounded with energy and life. The white-haired old men from Sfakia dancing on the holidays, their bodies grown stiff and brittle to bend like ancient bows but still possessed of an awesome grace. The Cretan girls, hair black as raven's wings, faces serene as madonnas even as their bodies moved with concupiscent flame. And where they walked, the old women, eyelids sprinkled by black sand, hovered nearby. In their timeless knowledge of suffering in a world of men, from the pain of recurrent childbirth, to the toil that thickened and wearied their bodies and spirits, they knew youth, beauty, and love would all someday settle in the inexpiable embrace of death.

What does it mean to say that one's roots are sprung in a particular section of the earth? Are not countries much the same, trees and mountains, sea and sky? What foolishness to claim greater resonance for one patch above all others. From such allegiance bursts the madness of war. Yet, from the love of his land, a poet's song comes as well. Near the end of his life, Nikos Kazantzakis, the greatest of the modern Greeks, could write of his island birthplace in this way:

"I hold this Cretan soil and squeeze it with ineffable joy, tenderness and gratitude as though in my hand I were squeezing the breast of a woman I loved and bidding it farewell. This soil I was everlastingly, this soil I shall be everlastingly. O fierce clay of Crete, the moment when you were twirled and fashioned into a man of struggle has passed in a flash."

An enigma for me in my childhood, the feeling of exile and separation from a land I had never seen, and an enigma for me now. For until I understand I am not sure where I belong. Born in Missouri, America my home, the island Crete remains to haunt me. Perhaps that is the way it will always be.

From this island, Crete, my father and mother with four of my older brothers and sisters emigrated to the United States in 1916.

I

I HAVE SEEN an old brown and faded photograph
of my father and mother with four of my
brothers and sisters, a photograph taken a few
months before they came to America. My father sits
imposingly in a large, highbacked chair resembling
a Minoan throne, my mother and the children clustered around him. He wears a tall black stovepipe
hat, common to Greek Orthodox priests of that period
of the First World War, and a long black cassock
covering him from neck to ankles. Even seated he
gives the impression of height and strength. Above
the glossy abundance of his beard, a quality of arrogance molds his face. He was thirty years old when
the photo was taken, in splendid health, and pos-
sessing an unflinching conviction that he had been
consecrated to elevate the lance and the cup and the
Holy Grail containing the ever-fresh blood of the
Saviour. He had not yet been assailed by illness and
age, and was still unblighted by the dark knowledge

15

that if a divinity shaped our ends, that divinity might still be powerless against injustice.

My mother is a small, handsome woman with thick long hair swept back into a bun and bound with a pair of pearl-rimmed combs. The combs are not visible in the photograph, but having seen them often later, and having been told by my mother that she brought them from Crete, I know they must be there securing the soft, heavy strands of her hair. (As a child I took them once from her dresser and with a strange warm excitement slipped them into my own hair where they glittered like a pair of small fragile wings.)

But most significant are my mother's eyes. Despite the four children she had borne, her eyes in the photograph exhibit an innocence, a serenity curiously remote from the shadows and tensions I remember years later. Her eyes changed as she traced a furrow in suffering in the way a farmer traces a furrow in a field.

My mother's maiden name was Christoulakis, and she came from the village of Nipos not far from Rethymnon in Central Crete. Before she was born her parents had three children, two girls and a boy. All three died before they reached the age of three. When my grandmother became pregnant for the fourth time, carrying my mother, she and my grandfather prayed fervently that if the child lived they would consecrate its life to St. Stellianou (Stanley or Stella) and offer an icon to the church in honor of the saint. My mother was born and they christened her Stella.

The threat of early death seemed about to repeat itself once more. When my mother was about two, she became seriously ill. Crete had few doctors, but my grandfather heard of a French physician visiting in Rethymnon. He traveled by horseback to the city and pleaded with the doctor to alleviate the malady that devoured his children. The doctor, moved by my grandfather's pleas, returned to Nipos with him and diagnosed my mother's illness as typhoid fever. He offered scant hope that the child would survive.

My grandparents prayed to my mother's patron saint and placed small icons in the four corners of the child's sickroom.

The entire village took up the cause. An icon of St. Luke in a nearby monastery was reported to have supernatural powers. A petition was presented to the Turkish governor in Rethymnon for permission to carry the icon to my grandparents' house. Permission was granted and early one morning, led by a priest and a coterie of acolytes, everyone in the village able to walk moved in a chanting procession to the monastery. They carried the icon back to my mother's room. While the villagers assembled around the

17

house and prayed, my grandfather raised my mother in his arms.

"Come, child, kiss the icon and it will make you well." My mother claims to this day she remembers those words spoken to her, and the cool feel of the icon under her lips. Afterwards, miraculously, she recovered. (Through the power of the icon and my grandparents' faith, my mother says.)

My father's grandparents came from the province of Sfakia, one of the most rugged and inaccessible regions of Crete, a place of stark gorges and steep canyons. Under Venetians and, later, Turks, the Sfakians remained their own law. They descended in bands to raid the foreign garrisons and then retreated to their mountain strongholds, setting up ambushes for any troops foolish enough to pursue them. They were like a tribe of pagan warriors, constantly at war, living by brigandage, smuggling, and piracy. When they were not raiding and harassing Turks, with equability they plundered villages of other Cretans, or fought and killed each other in vendettas as bloody and savage as those of Sicily and Corsica.

By the end of the nineteenth century the unceasing rebellions, warfare, blood feuds had decimated many of the families. The arable land had been laid waste, the flocks scattered, houses left in ruins. Infelicity and bitterness drove families to emigrate to other sections of Crete. In one such move my grand-parents settled in the village of Villandredou, a fertile, sun-soaked oasis high in the mountains above Rethymnon.

My father, one of five children, removed from the environment of vendettas and warfare, funneled his energies into still another battleground. He studied for the priesthood, completing his theological studies in Rethymnon. Afterwards, caught for a moment by uncertainty, he delayed his ordainment, considering as an alternative studying music, because he had a strong, resonant voice.

When the Bishop of Rethymnon learned of my father's hesitation, he called him into private council and reminded him sternly that the Orthodox Church had been the means by which the faith, tradition, and language had survived under the Venetians, Franks, and Turks. Seeking a life outside the church, the Bishop said, meant my father was shirking his sacred responsibilities to his land, family, and the hallowed dead. As for his voice, bestowed upon him as it had been by God, the Bishop said, let my father use it in the chanting of hymns to the glory of God.

Ashamed of his contemplated dereliction, my father agreed to accept ordainment. Since young men entering the priesthood were only permitted to marry if they did so before ordainment, the Bishop recom-

19

mended a lovely girl from a prosperous family that, by sheer chance, happened to be related to him.

My father did not have anyone special in mind and trusted the matchmaking propensities of his prelate. But the capricious belle (missing her chance to become my mother) would have none of the shabby habiliments associated with a parish priest's wife and vehemently refused.

The Bishop was outraged, but unwilling to surrender a reliable prospective bastion of Orthodoxy, settled quickly upon Stella Christoulakis, now seventeen years old. He wrote the young girl's father (a first cousin of the Bishop) asking him to anticipate the visit of a young man named Mark Petrakis, of a reputable family and destined for the service of God. Still rankling over the earlier rejection, he included a somber warning about the shortage of eligible young men and the emotional instability of young girls grievously infected by the cursed epidemic of French novels.

Less than a week later, my father, accompanied by a close friend, traveled on horseback to the village of Nipos. After stabling their horses they sent word, respectfully, to my mother's father, asking to be received. My grandfather formally invited them into his parlor, spoke of various inconsequential topics, when my mother entered carrying a tray of coffee and sweet loukoumi. Neither my father nor my mother appeared to have been struck by love at first sight.

"She was very short," my father said, years later, about his first impression of my mother. "The top of her head would not have reached my armpit. And she had a certain defiant air that suggested trouble for any man who gave her orders. But she had an attractive face and fine thick hair. I thought she would do as well as any other girl."

"He was tall and very thin," my mother recalled. "With a countenance like a mournful deacon. It was as if a smile cost him money. But he was very polite and had sensitive eyes. I thought a few years of good meals would fill him out."

That evening the engagement was sealed pending the drawing up of an acceptable dowry.

I have seen the faded and worn marriage contract that in formal and stilted language transferred to my father 2000 gold drachmas, an orchard of 37 olive trees, free and clear of debt, some adjoining orange and peach trees, and assorted household items, bedding, spreads, pots and pans, knives and forks. In addition he received my mother. They were married in the spring of 1908, and my father accepted ordainment shortly afterwards.

After my parents married they lived in the city of Rethymnon for the following seven years. The first children were born and, true to her pledge, my mother's cooking put meat on my father's lean frame. He served as priest to a small, prosperous parish where he was respected for his resoluteness and praised for his marvelous voice. Men and women came from outlying villages to hear him sing the troparia on Sunday mornings.

I never heard my father's magnificent voice. When I was less than six months old and we were living in St. Louis, he developed a nasal obstruction and had an operation. His voice was never the same. In the upper registers it lost its strength and became a kind of reedy wail (God punishing him for vanity, an old virago once wrote him vehemently).

In 1898, the Allied Powers, culminating decades of machinations and intrigues, forced the Turks to leave Crete and granted the island autonomous status. Finally, in 1913, Crete was united with Greece. But the blood-wounds of the abortive uprisings, the passions and the rivalries, had left the island poor and scarred. The first migrations of Greeks began settling in America, and the letters they wrote back to their towns and villages glowed with the marvels of the new land.

In 1916, Europe aflame with war, my father was offered a parish in Price, Utah, a coal-mining community with many young Greek immigrants working in the mines. My father might have been content to remain in Crete, but he knew that America would provide a better education for his children. He considered the offer carefully, discussed it with my mother, and finally, not without some apprehension and anguish, accepted. They made ready to leave for the long journey. He did not realize then that he would never return to Crete again.

The night of their arrival in America, they were detained on Ellis Island by the immigration authorities because the Greek church official from the community in Utah had not arrived. My father was embittered and angered at the separation of his family into the male and female compounds. In his fury he broke a chain bearing a gold coin from around his throat. Before the immigration officials he bit at the coin to confirm its purity and offered it to them as a bond for the admission of his family.

In later years he spoke of lying awake through that long unhappy night listening to the snores and mutterings of immigrants sleeping in cots around him. He would laugh wryly and assert that was his first pungent introduction to democracy, the first substantive lesson to his venerable, bearded, and cassocked old-country pride.

My family remained in Price for two years and were then transferred to a parish in Savannah, Georgia.

Three years after moving to Savannah, my father moved once again to St. Louis, Missouri. In 1923,

II

I SEEM to forever remember streets of matching brick three-story apartment buildings, all with cramped-as-kangaroo-pouch entrances, and the windows veiled by flimsy, gossamer curtains. Separating the buildings were narrow gangways the sun never touched, leading into grassless back yards littered with scraps of old newspapers. A maze of porches with paint peeling from the wood hung in tiers above the yards. At dawn, the milkmen jingled and clinked their bottles on the stairs, and in the twilight the janitors lumbered up and down carrying the huge containers strapped to their backs into which they emptied the waste from the garbage cans. Standing like ragged kings on the landings of the porches, we surveyed the landscape of our domain, numerous identical porches and below them desolate, crumbling garages flanking the oil-soaked and turd-spattered alleys.

These were the reservations of the city where we lived wedged together, Poles and Lithuanians, Irish and Germans, Greeks and Jews. We had no common bond except that which we shared as the sons and daughters of parents who had forsaken their homelands and through successive years sought to retain what they feared they might lose when they became the uprooted. For each of us, as children, the city existed only as a province of the land from which our parents journeyed.

My earliest memories, tangled and ambulatory, had to do with what was almost totally Greek. Greek parents, Greek language, Greek food, Greek school, and Greek church. There were artifacts that belonged to the new land—candy and baseball, ice cream and movies. For the most part these existed as a kind of exotic bazaar outside the gates of the real city in which I lived.

Since we were a large family, my father, mother, Naka, who took care of us, and her son, five of my brothers and sisters and myself, the ten of us needed at least seven rooms, and even with that amount of space, we were cramped. The layout of the succession of flats we rented was invariably the same. The kitchen was at one end, and the living room at the other end. Connecting them was a long narrow hallway from which a series of doors opened into small dark bedrooms with a single window that looked out over the gangways at bedroom or bathroom windows across the way. In one or two of the half-dozen apartments we lived in over these years there were also sun parlors graced by windows on three sides.

The furniture that we moved from apartment to apartment consisted of certain indestructible items that never seemed to wear out. There was a ponderous bulky sofa that opened into a bed on which I slept for a number of years. When we had company in the evening, my older brothers and sisters entertaining their friends, I went to sleep in one of the bedrooms. After the guests had departed and the couch opened, I was wakened and walked sleepily from the bedroom to the living room. In the morning, after I was up, the bed was closed, the cushions replaced, and not a trace left of my nightly sojourn. This disappearing bed provided me the tenuous, uneasy status of a boarder.

There was a dining-room table, a sturdy monster of heavy walnut which opened to accept three additional leaves. On this table we ate our meals, did our homework, and played Ping-Pong. The edges of the wood became chipped and the surface scarred and stained, but with a clean tablecloth spread across its full length, the table assumed a majestic elegance.

There were six chairs that belonged to the table, one of them an armchair, which was always placed at the head of the table for my father. That chair had one of its arms broken for almost fifteen years. We tried to cement it many times, but wear would loosen

27

the mucilage and a day always came when my father would sit down in the chair, bend his head to say grace, and afterwards sit back grasping the arms of the chair to pull himself closer to the table. The broken arm fell off to the floor. From my childhood into my adolescence I recall my father sighing with resignation as he looked grimly around the table at his silent sons and daughters.

"If one of you," he'd say slowly, making an effort to be patient, "if just one of you would give up planning to become millionaires or philosophers and study a little carpentry . . ."

He'd reach down and pick up the arm and replace it on the chair. He ate the balance of the meal leaning slightly to one side, while the rest of us pledged anew our determination to make a permanent repair.

We had an old upright player piano that was hauled from third-floor apartment to third-floor apartment accompanied by the groans and curses of the movers. There were dozens of roles of music for the spindle. I loved to play the rolls, imagining I was a brilliant concert pianist, my feet pumping wildly, and my hands and fingers flashing along the keys. Over the holidays the piano played a more conventional role when one of my sisters, Barbara or Tasula, played her repertoire of old favorites and the family gathered about her to sing loudly if not well.

The day in our house began early, with my brothers and sisters snatching pieces of toast and gulping a few sips of coffee or milk before leaving for colleges or jobs. My sister Irene and I, both in elementary school, ate more leisurely. Because our time of departure generally coincided with that of my father, the three of us usually ate breakfast together. He had certain table requirements that Naka rigidly observed. Regardless of whether a tablecloth was already spread on the table, a clean linen napkin would be opened before his place. On the napkin would be his bowl of dry cornflakes, a pitcher of cream, knife, fork, and napkin, a cup for coffee or tea, and, because he was a diabetic, a small container with saccharin. When he had finished his cereal, Naka would bring him his eggs, which had been boiled for exactly three minutes.

After breakfast, my sister and I walked beside my father clad in his black coat, black hat, white clerical collar glistening around his throat, down 61st Street toward Michigan Avenue where the parish church and school were located. The storekeepers (mostly Jewish immigrants) sweeping their walks and opening their stores would greet my father's tall, dark figure with respect, bowing in an old-country courtliness that overflowed across my stiff, proud shoulders as well.

On Sunday mornings our ritual was altered. My father would wake me early and I would dress in my best and only suit and the two of us would walk to church along the streets of the sleeping city. The windows of the stores were shaded and still, only the sound of our steps sharp and clear off the silent pavements. Now and then a prowling tomcat marked our passage with a baleful eye.

When we unlocked the door and entered the church, it would be cold and bleak with the dampness of the night. In a short while the sexton would begin to light the myriad candles before the icons of the white-bearded, fierce-eyed saints. I'd assist my brother Manuel as he helped my father into his vestments, the two of us binding the bright, beaded layers of cloth, cord, and ribbons. Afterwards I'd hurry to join the white-robed altar boys sitting with their arms folded and their lips tightly sealed under the ominous eye of my oldest brother, Dan. He was an athlete, strong, agile, and swift in baseball, basketball, and track. The sport at which he truly excelled, however, was the reverberant slapping of our heads at the slightest infraction of his rules. Hard as I tried to keep my conduct exemplary to avoid his swinging injunctions, I was slapped more than any boy at the altar. This action was necessary, he patiently explained to me at home, to prevent any possible accusation of favoritism. I felt ardently that such estimable fairness should be rewarded, and many nights I grimly pondered ways to properly repay him for his zeal.

As the time approached for the start of the liturgy, the church blazed with the warmth and flame of hundreds of candles. The black-gowned, white-collared girls of the choir clustered before the stately choirmaster, listening attentively to his final whispered instructions.

When I was young, I saw the parishioners who filled the church simply as a crowd of blurred faces, without separate identity. As I grew older I began to apportion differences to them. In the front pews, closest to the sanctuary, the oldest and most infirm men and women sat, regarding the ornaments of the liturgy somberly, without a fragment of pleasure or joy. Their attentive faces reflected the anguished questions in their minds. Would the balance sheet of their lives permit them entry into the city of God? Was it reasonable to take solace in piety and assurance in faith?

After them, the middle-aged men and women entered and took places in the pews. These were fathers and mothers who had lived more than half their lives, whose children were grown with scant patience for parental counsel any more. Strange longings and fitful pains assailed them, sometimes their nights were troubled and sleepless, and they were unable to

31

dispel the dark awareness of time as a clock that never paused and never missed a beat.

The young married couples entered church with babies squirming in their arms, babies whose shrill voices cried out like flutes on scattered islands. In the intervals when they were not soothing the infants, the young parents would proffer their devotions a little impatiently while making plans for the things to be done after church.

Finally, when the Sunday School classes marched into church for the last hour of the service, there would be added to the congregation young boys and girls, secured to their seats by the eyelocks of stern teachers. They radiated the arrogance of youth, the courage of innocence, and the security of good health.

At the end of the service, the girls of the choir, my sisters among them, would file past my father to receive a piece of the bread of the sacrament. Then, pew by pew, the congregation would rise, make two lines on each side of the church and walk slowly toward the altar to kiss my father's hand and receive the bread. By the time the last of the parishioners had passed, my father's cheeks were damp with perspiration, his brocaded vestments glittering with the reflection of the candles.

When we returned home after church on Sundays, we would have the main meal of our week, a festive dinner that often served, in addition to the family, visiting priests, theological students, young Talmudists, commercial travelers, all setting their feet with anticipation under my mother's table. For although Naka cooked many of the meals at our house during the week, it was understood that Sunday dinner belonged to my mother.

I, early in my life, accepted and understood the miracle of the multiplying loaves and fishes, since whether there were fifteen, twenty, or twenty-five visitors gathered at our table for that Sunday dinner, my mother fed us all a savory and abundant meal. She accomplished this despite the fact that her household budget could rarely afford more meat for the dinner than a pair of meager chickens. But, with rampant guile, she prepared great pans of pilaf, the succulent, steaming rice garnished with a redolent tomato sauce. We ate plate after plate of pilaf, until we were full to bursting. And we did not feel deprived, for within the mounds of rice, small slivers of chicken glittered, confirming that there had been meat on the menu as well.

After the meal, the men loosened their belts and lit cigars. My sisters served small cups of sweet "Turkish" coffee, the delicacy chauvinistic Greeks called "Greek" coffee. There were also tiny glasses of ouzo and cognac, and the syrupy honey-nut baklava. In thick, spiraling columns of smoke and nectareous mist, the discussion and debate began. Philosophy, politics, and social revolution were all given free play, since these were the first years of the Franklin Roosevelt administration, the New Deal, and the N.R.A. There were manifold things on which to disagree.

When we moved from politics to religion, my brother and sister who were students at the University of Chicago sharpened their knives as if they were zealous apprentices in a butcher shop with a fresh shipment of beef on the block. My father, smiling in his chair at the head of the table, would finally let them loose.

The words and arguments flew up from the table like feathers being plucked from startled chickens. After a while a harried priest or theology student assaulted by my sister's and brother's cries for reason and scientific truth might turn to ask my father how he condoned heresy and agnosticism in his house.

"Democracy," my father would shrug with a wry smile. "That's the trouble here, democracy."

Our neighborhood was a city within a city bounded by the walls of our streets. We knew there was an area called "downtown," made infrequent trips there with one of our parents, knew there was a North Side (home of the ritzy Cub fans) and a West Side, but for all the relevance these sections had for us, they might have been cities in Europe.

There was a tangible smell to our neighborhood, a warmth and reassurance in recognizable faces and sociable friends. I walked delightedly along our street at twilight, watching the lights from the windows throw their misted gleam across the walks. I knew who lived in each of the apartments. There was a basement flat where the husky German janitor lived, a curtained sanctuary of bacchanalian revels with the janitor and his friends singing boisterous drinking songs. Late at night their voices grew low and husky with nostalgia for the Black Forest and the Rhine. In a first-floor apartment a few doors from our own building lived my friend Marvin Salant, our friendship begun years before in an argument over our tricycles. In the middle of the block was the two-flat where the Asher sisters lived. Bernice and Florence, names that will forever connote for me those dark-eyed and black-haired beauties who graced our block with a basaltic elegance.

There were the storekeepers in the shops along the street that my sister, my father, and I walked on our way to church. Sometimes, after school was out, I visited them with my mother.

There was Belson's grocery, a neat, clean store with the fruits and vegetables stacked in careful tiers. Max Belson himself came to wait on my mother, the wife of the respected Greek priest.

"How much for this lettuce, Mr. Belson?" my

mother would ask. This question she accompanied by holding the lettuce gingerly in her hand, involving it precariously on the scales of her decision. Max Belson would look at her with the suffering visage of a man who heard too many similar questions too many times.

Whatever the daily price he quoted my mother, her response was always the same. With the fervor of a tragic chorus she'd emit a low moan and drop the lettuce back on the pile where it seemed to shrivel in shame. Max Belson calmly smoothed the ruffled leaf.

"Your price, Mrs. Petrakis, you tell me. You tell Belson what you think it's worth."

But my mother would not be drawn into that artful game and had already swept on to the tomatoes, to do battle over still another patch of produce, until the fortifications were breached by a dozen deployments and the defender so distracted he could not be sure where or on what item the final major assault would come.

There was a delicatessen run by a man with the euphonious name of Morris Satin. I can remember the pungent kosher scents when I stepped inside, the trays of glistening scarlet and pearl corned beef, pepper-riddled pastrami, and great swarthy pickles soaking in barrels of brine.

There was a magazine store with long racks of

pulp magazines (before the days of the pocket book and TV) and the tall, thin dark-haired owner whose name escapes me now. At an early age I sought to expand my libidinal horizons by purchasing an occasional copy of *Spicy Western* stories. (That was the real West.) When I had selected the magazine from one of his racks and carried it to the register where he waited for me to pay him the quarter, our dialogue never varied.

"Does your father know you're buying magazines like this?" he asked.

"They're for my older brother," I said, looking at the tips of my scuffed shoes.

That was not true and he knew it, but the identical question and answer each time satisfied the moral proprieties and assuaged whatever slight proddings of conscience he felt.

Farther along the street was a tiny candy store, the narrow space inside the door filled by a counter of jelly beans, spice drops, and a few varieties of hand-made chocolates. Almost filling the area between the counter and the door was a popcorn and caramel corn stand. The owner, a gentle, mild-voiced little Greek who lavished as much courtesy on a penny customer as he did on the dollar purchaser of his chocolates, drew almost all his trade from people attending the small neighborhood show next door.

During the Depression the show was sold to a pair

37

of enterprising men, strangers from the North Side, and they quickly installed a candy counter and popcorn machine of their own. After that, the candy store closed down. For a long time, when I passed the abandoned store, the Coke placard in the window faded more deeply into the dust.

But remorse did not prevent me from going to work for those same ruthless violators of small business. I joined fifteen other ten- and eleven-year-olds an hour after school, two afternoons a week, stuffing the show's prevue handbills into neighborhood mailboxes. Because the owners were suspicious men, we were regularly pursued by a half-dozen older boys, hired as finks, to assure we did not dump our handbills into the first convenient garbage can.

Our salary came in the form of one free admission apiece to a regular showing. On Saturday afternoons, pursuers and pursued would be grouped together in a roped-off area in the lobby of the theater, while the prosperous children who paid cash for their admission tickets walked briskly past us. Only after the film, a Tim Holt or Buck Jones Western, or a Laurel and Hardy comedy, had run about ten minutes were we allowed to file quietly to our assigned rows in the back of the theater. Those ten minutes that we waited after the picture started and we could hear the sounds from within the darkened theater were among the most agonizing moments of my childhood.

If one traveled west from our neighborhood, across Cottage Grove Avenue, to the location of my father's church, the district was almost completely Negro, Cottage Grove being the dividing line. The church included our parish school, which taught English subjects from 9 to 12:30 and, after a break for lunch, Greek grammar and history from 1 until 3.

Our teachers were both Greek and American, and achieved a common ethnic denominator by their reliance upon the stick. Hardly a class passed without someone getting walloped. As a rule, the American teachers struck without any great conviction, but the Greek teachers struck with a rampant fervor.

We had boys in our class who, for continued infractions, received most of the punishment. There was one swift classmate of mine who when threatened with a beating would sprint to a rear window, open it, and leap through a second before the outraged teacher reached him. He was called "The Racer." We had another boy called, for obvious reasons, "The Howler." At the first blow, however light, he would begin to howl and shriek in unremitting agony, rolling his eyes, clutching his head. There was still another boy called "The Dodger," for his gymnastic ability. As supple as a snake, he would twist and coil

39

his body, neatly evading most of the violent flailings of the stick. We watched these bouts with rapt admiration until the exhausted teacher gave up, having failed to land more than two or three blows out of thirty.

My own experience with the stick included a period when for some reason I was never struck. "You never get hit 'cause your father's the priest," classmates told me resentfully. There was another interminable period when I suffered the cursed stick for the most trivial infraction. "You always get hit 'cause your father's the priest," classmates told me consolingly.

Across the street from our church and school was a Roman Catholic church and parish school. That was a foreign country ruled by long-black-skirted, white-cowled sisters with the awesome capability to deliver bare-handed blows that equaled the force of the ones struck by our teachers with sticks. I once witnessed a boy pulled out of line by an irate sister who held him by the scruff of his jacket and then delivered a short, fierce blow to the side of his head. The boy landed crumpled against the fence, apparently out cold. It was a knockout Jack Dempsey would have envied.

Reflecting the neighborhood, most of the students in the Catholic school were Negroes. We came as interlopers from the white neighborhood across Cottage Grove. Black and white, we were mortal enemies, constantly at war. Our assaults and forays against one another ranged from curses and stone-throwing to full-scale battles with fists and sticks. I cannot remember anyone getting killed, which was a wonder considering the number of broken teeth and bloody heads. After such encounters our teachers pulled us inside and beat us, much as the Negro boys were being beaten across the street. The punishment served only to intensify our fury.

There was a Negro boy I will never forget, tall and strong, although he was no more than fourteen, with the speed and body of a superb athlete, who spread terror among us. The sight of his flashing eyes and great white teeth bared in a scream of battle struck us with panic. One ignominious day he hurtled the fence to enter our playground, and a hundred of us, boys and girls caught in some mob fear, fled frantically for the protection of our school buildings. The spectacle of that boy, all alone, chasing a hundred of us into the school remains with me to this day.

But our most disgraceful battles, organized and led by older boys, were reserved for Halloween. By twilight on that day we would have armed ourselves with overripe tomatoes, bottles, and sticks, and after dark, in gangs of fifty or more, we'd move into the

41

alleys across Cottage Grove. Meanwhile, gangs of black youths would be foraging through our alleys, searching us out. Sometimes there were brief, preliminary skirmishes by patrols of a few boys, but ultimately the main forces were joined, the battle becoming a massive, tangled melee of bodies and missiles flying in the darkness. I was one of the younger boys, fighting in the rear ranks, and since it was impossible to distinguish friend or foe, we threw our tomatoes and bottles at random. We must have struck our own boys as often as we hit those of the other side. But this dereliction was equaled by the fact that our antagonists were doing the same thing.

In the basements afterwards where we retired to wash and dress our bruises before returning to our homes, a wound was a wound, whether inflicted by friend or foe. Shamefully, ignorantly, we felt a primal pride in the scars of battle.

Where are they now? The boys I played with, the girls I walked beside? Where are the young Negroes we fought in the senseless, dupable bigotry of our youth? Where is the black Achilles who struck such terror in my heart? Where are "The Racer," "The Howler," "The Dodger"? Do they still meet the assaults of life as they once met the attacks of angry teachers?

Where is Belson, who suffered with patience and

fortitude the daily assault of a hundred determined women? Where are the cruel men (invaders from the far North Side) who made us wait those frantic ten minutes on Saturday afternoons? Where are the store-keepers who greeted us each morning as my sister and I walked proudly beside my father on our way to school?

I know where my father is. He is dead now and lies straight and still beneath a flowered patch of cemetery sod. How many of the others must be dead, too, their sons and daughters scattered across the country and the world, remembering even as I remember now?

If I could I would say to them, this is the way it was on those crisp mornings in autumn when we scuffed our sneakers through the brown, wrinkled leaves; those afternoons in early spring, the windows of our classrooms open to the scent of new buds; those twilights in the summer with the mothers calling plaintively as we crouched hidden in the shadows.

For we shared this kingdom of our childhood, lived there as sprinters and fools, first learned of joy and sorrow, played against time in games we always won, and felt no dread of age and death.

And thought the sun would remain young forever . . .

III

M Y FATHER was an imposing figure to me as he moved about the sanctuary in church on Sunday mornings. The candles and the cross reflected on his vestments so that he radiated the majesty of a Byzantine king. Although he could be gentle and warm as well as stern and demanding, there was an irrevocable dignity about him. He was no ivory-tower cleric, but a man with a good deal of common sense. Few of his enemies in the councils of the parish made the error of underestimating him more than once. Even those who had felt the sting of his censure accorded him an unreserved respect.

Only my mother seemed to lag behind in the procession of adulation that followed my father. By her unwritten articles of dissent she implied that behind his revered presence, his imposing demeanor, his eloquence and gift for laughter, a man with foibles and intemperate pride existed, as well. He was, she said, for all of his epiphanies, a mortal, and she zealously reminded him of this simple fact.

Sometime in the early years of their marriage, for reasons which remain unknown to me, my father and mother began a resolute and unyielding struggle to impose their will upon one another. When this battle achieved only a stalemate, neither side able to assert any dominance, they divided their efforts and activities, doing what they wanted without consulting each other. Neither would compromise their position and for all the years I can remember they remained antipodal points on a compass.

Nowhere was this rivalry more clearly revealed than during the dinners we ate with guests assembled at our long dining-room table. My father sat at one end, his lambent brown eyes and fluent voice charming the guests about him with a story. He'd smile a crooked little curling of his lips, lower his voice to heighten suspense, gesture with his slender, mobile fingers, and then finish with animation. Men and women responded like a chorus of woodwinds and brasses. My father laughed delightedly with them until, as their appreciative mirth crested and declined, he picked up my mother's voice carrying an independent melody from within the circle of guests gathered at the other end of the table.

If my father was the orchestra conductor, my mother was the coloratura soprano, a defiant, talented, and persuasive artist in her own right. Because she was less than five feet tall, she'd always tilt her

45

chair forward, sitting on the edge, so her toes could reach the floor. From this vantage point she cajoled her coterie of listeners, enchanting them with a pithy text of her own. She had a quick, lilting voice, full of ripples, breakers, and billows and flecked with a wry penetrating humor. As my father dominated one end of the table, my mother prevailed at the other end.

For a small woman, my mother had an incredible abundance of energy and strength. A certain rampant force of life within her drove her forward. She had no fear of the before and the after, of the above and the below, of this world or the world to come. Her faith was the wellspring from which she drew certainty.

She believed firmly that God held the earth in His eyes. Using her faith as a compass, she charted the undeviating course of her life. All roads led to service. She founded, directed, and helped sustain numerous organizations within the parish. Given blocks of tickets for a community raffle or picnic, she outsold everyone else, disposing of the pile with equanimity to willing and unwilling purchasers. Storekeepers fled out the rear doors when they saw her entering. They need not have bothered, because she would invariably return. A strong believer in the parity of religions, she did not solicit ads for a church program book from Christians alone, but adeptly canvassed Jews, Moslems, and agnostics as well. In the areas outside the church she worked like a zealot for the Red Cross, Community Fund, Interfaith group, and hospital auxiliaries.

Her most ingenious efforts involved helping individuals whose suffering and misfortunes had been overlooked by the church or social agencies. She developed a network of women across the city who brought these cases to her attention. For one crippled old man she gained admission into Oak Forest, the county home. For an ailing mother with young children she obtained regular delivery of free bread, eggs, butter, and milk. For an old woman without any means of support she obtained a pension. For another woman, whose son had been caught in an attempted robbery, she procured legal counsel for the boy and appeared herself as a witness on his behalf.

There were also times my mother was called upon to act as a marriage broker, a role she played with artful cunning and delight. She approached each connubial crucible as if the survival of the race depended upon her making the match. When she managed to bring a man and woman together, her only reward, usually, was the gratefulness of the parents and, sometimes, being asked to become godmother to the couple's first child. After many years of successful matchmaking, my mother had two score children calling her "Nouna."

Sometimes my mother's zeal prodded her into areas where her help was not solicited and not infrequently was resented. Hearing of a feud or quarrel between families in the parish, she'd wangle a meeting between the dissidents and earnestly seek to establish a common ground for reconciliation. My father conceded there had been a few reconciliations attributable to my mother's efforts. These came about, he said, because my mother's relentless quest for peace produced such distress in the dissidents that peace was the only method by which they could eliminate my mother's intervention.

My father, sometimes ruefully, acknowledged the benefits of my mother's labors. At the same time he wished fervently she would exercise certain restraints. She had slight patience with the evasive maneuverings of affluent parishioners she approached for help, or the ceremonial forms and courtesies practiced by the protocol-riddled vice presidents of parish organizations. Often when one of these men or women had been subjected to my mother's bold importunings, they'd complain angrily to my father. My father would bitterly accuse my mother of eroding the carefully wrought structure of diplomacy he had erected. He understood to a much greater degree than my mother the necessities of compromise and negotiation to achieve results. He'd try patiently to explain these things to her. But my mother could not be prevailed upon to operate by means of soporific courtesies or committees. She wished my father were less like Disraeli and more like Luther.

"When things need correction, an effort should be made to correct them at once," she said. "When people need help, they must be helped at once. Hunger doesn't wait for societies to take a vote. Illness doesn't wait for a formal delegation."

I came to understand that my father, like an assured and dedicated surgeon, sought to remain objective as he performed the ministrations of charity. My mother scorned detachment, involving herself with all kinds of people who pursued her, pleaded with her, plagued her. Deserving and undeserving, she made an effort to help them all. While my father solicited order in his life and harmony in his surroundings, my mother thrived on disorder. My father considered conventional channels of charity conserved energy and minimized the possibilities for abuses. My mother hastily assembled her own artifacts of assistance. If most people were repelled at the sight of stark suffering and decay, my mother fearlessly touched the festered sores of sickness and the wounds of anguish. Sometimes, it was true, as

49

my father said, that she was duped and gulled. She simply could not ignore a cry for help.

During these Depression years of the 1930s, hardship existed in families all around us. My father's salary kept slipping until it barely managed to cover the basic food and housing needs of the ten people in our house. Gas, phone, and electric bills were outposts perpetually under siege.

My sisters and brothers worked at part-time jobs to help with their school expenses. The most difficult task fell upon my mother. From the small household allowance given to her by my father, she had to perform an economic wizardry. In the neighborhood groceries and meat markets she was feared and respected as a ruthless bargainer. She stubbornly walked an additional three blocks to save ten cents on some item.

When she managed to cover our food needs for the week, there were still those emergencies when one of her children went to her with a desperate request for money to buy pants or a pair of silk stockings. We were reluctant to ask my father but, somehow, my mother scraped together what was needed. I think she accomplished these feats by paring her own personal expenses to the bone. She never went to a beauty shop in her life and wore her dresses and hats and coats until they were shabby and worn out. Regardless of the thrift she practiced, my father felt somehow that my mother's whirl of activities outside the house added to our financial hardship. In addition he felt we were being deprived of a warm and maternal environment in our home. But although she was willing to make personal sacrifices, my mother refused to limit her role to consoling her children and balancing her household accounts. She was more vitally concerned with the accounting she would have to make someday to God.

In this way my parents continued for years to live and work divided. For better or worse this division fashioned their achievements and left unresolved whatever benefits might have accrued from a placid and unchallenged union. Sometimes they worked toward the same goal, but these truces never lasted for long. Some indefinable core of unyielding strength in each of them, some wellspring of identity they had to maintain, kept them alienated. When there were no longer new grievances to muster, they'd spend hours recounting the old complaints to their sons and daughters.

"If your mother had not been so stubborn," my father said.

"If your father had been more understanding," my mother said.

51

"She could have helped me in so many ways," my father said.

"He would not let me help him," my mother said.

In the last few years of my father's life, when illness had weakened him and enemies snapped at his heels, my mother joined her force to my father again. Like vigorous and tenacious roots of a single great tree that had existed apart for decades, their strengths were merged once more. But they were no longer young, the years had scarred and wearied them, and all they could do in the end was to suffer with and try to console one another.

When my father entered the hospital for the last three months of his life, my mother remained with him from early in the morning until late at night, tending to his needs, shielding him from overzealous friends. She read to him for hours, told him of events taking place in the community, endured his querulous complaints, his pain, and his resignation. As his strength declined, she made a mighty, futile effort to bind him to life. They grew closer, I think, in those days than they had been since the early years of their marriage. And, sometimes, as he silently watched her, or she stared at him while he lay asleep, there was a sense of remorse, a plea for forgiveness, the mute placing of a seal once more upon their hearts.

When his family and friends mourned prematurely, my mother spoke with conviction of my father's strength and will evidenced many times over the years. She accepted without our awe his capacity, time and time again, to fight back from the precipice of death.

"I know this man better than any of you," she said to us impatiently. "When he assembles his spirit, he has the strength of five men. He has given his years to God, and God will not forsake him."

But my father's strength and spirit, worn by illness and grief, finally drained away. He died late one night in his sleep less than an hour after my mother had left the hospital. When I returned with her to the hospital, a nurse took us into his room. My father lay still in death, his arms along his sides, a narrow band of cloth around his head holding his mouth closed. My mother's face was burned with a terrible grief, and she stood beside his bed in silence looking down at him. "Now he is at peace," she said softly. "Now he is at peace." She touched his hand gently with her fingers and bent and kissed his lips for the first time I can ever remember in all the years we had lived together.

To this day I am not sure if right or wrong can be equated between them. Perhaps, like the table in our house at which they sat, there are simply two ends, one end that belonged to my father and the other end to my mother.

IV

THERE WAS one storekeeper I remember above all others in my youth. It was shortly before I became ill, spending a good portion of my time with a motley group of varied ethnic ancestry. We contended with one another to deride the customs of the old country. On our Saturday forays into neighborhoods beyond our own, to prove we were really Americans, we ate hot dogs and drank Cokes. If a boy didn't have ten cents for this repast he went hungry, for he dared not bring a sandwich from home made of the spiced meats our families ate.

One of our untamed games was to seek out the owner of a pushcart or a store, unmistakably an immigrant, and bedevil him with a chorus of insults and jeers. To prove allegiance to the gang it was necessary to reserve our fiercest malevolence for a storekeeper or peddler belonging to our own ethnic background.

For that reason I led a raid on the small, shabby

54

grocery of old Barba Nikos, a short, sinewy Greek who walked with a slight limp and sported a flaring, handlebar mustache.

We stood outside his store and dared him to come out. When he emerged to do battle, we plucked a few plums and peaches from the baskets on the sidewalk and retreated across the street to eat them while he watched. He waved a fist and hurled epithets at us in ornamental Greek.

Aware that my mettle was being tested, I raised my arm and threw my half-eaten plum at the old man. My aim was accurate and the plum struck him on the cheek. He shuddered and put his hand to the stain. He stared at me across the street, and although I could not see his eyes, I felt them sear my flesh. He turned and walked silently back into the store. The boys slapped my shoulders in admiration, but it was a hollow victory that rested like a stone in the pit of my stomach.

At twilight when we disbanded, I passed the grocery alone on my way home. There was a small light burning in the store and the shadow of the old man's body outlined against the glass. Goaded by remorse, I walked to the door and entered.

The old man moved from behind the narrow wooden counter and stared at me. I wanted to turn and flee, but by then it was too late. As he motioned

55

Harry Mark Petrakis

for me to come closer, I braced myself for a curse or a blow.

"You were the one," he said, finally, in a harsh voice.

I nodded mutely.

"Why did you come back?"

I stood there unable to answer.

"What's your name?"

"Haralambos," I said, speaking to him in Greek.

He looked at me in shock. "You are Greek!" he cried. "A Greek boy attacking a Greek grocer!" He stood appalled at the immensity of my crime. "All right," he said coldly. "You are here because you wish to make amends." His great mustache bristled in concentration. "Four plums, two peaches," he said. "That makes a total of 78 cents. Call it 75. Do you have 75 cents, boy?"

I shook my head.

"Then you will work it off," he said. "Fifteen cents an hour into 75 cents makes"—he paused—"five hours of work. Can you come here Saturday morning?"

"Yes," I said.

"Yes, Barba Nikos," he said sternly. "Show respect."

"Yes, Barba Nikos," I said.

"Saturday morning at eight o'clock," he said. "Now go home and say thanks in your prayers that

56

I did not loosen your impudent head with a solid smack on the ear." I needed no further urging and fled.

Saturday morning, still apprehensive, I returned to the store. I began by sweeping, raising clouds of dust in dark and hidden corners. I washed the windows, whipping the squeegee swiftly up and down the glass in a fever of fear that some member of the gang would see me. When I finished I hurried back inside.

For the balance of the morning I stacked cans, washed the counter, and dusted bottles of yellow wine. A few customers entered, and Barba Nikos served them. A little after twelve o'clock he locked the door so he could eat lunch. He cut himself a few slices of sausage, tore a large chunk from a loaf of crisp-crusted bread, and filled a small cup with a dozen black shiny olives floating in brine. He offered me the cup. I could not help myself and grimaced.

"You are a stupid boy," the old man said. "You are not really Greek, are you?"

"Yes, I am."

"You might be," he admitted grudgingly. "But you do not act Greek. Wrinkling your nose at these fine olives. Look around this store for a minute. What do you see?"

"Fruits and vegetables," I said. "Cheese and olives and things like that."

He stared at me with a massive scorn. "That's

57

what I mean," he said. "You are a bonehead. You don't understand that a whole nation and a people are in this store."

I looked uneasily toward the storeroom in the rear, almost expecting someone to emerge.

"What about olives?" he cut the air with a sweep of his arm. "There are olives of many shapes and colors. Pointed black ones from Kalamata, oval ones from Amphissa, pickled green olives and sharp tangy yellow ones. Achilles carried black olives to Troy and after a day of savage battle leading his Myrmidons, he'd rest and eat cheese and ripe black olives such as these right here. You have heard of Achilles, boy, haven't you?"

"Yes," I said.

"Yes, Barba Nikos."

"Yes, Barba Nikos," I said.

He motioned at the row of jars filled with varied spices. "There is origanon there and basilikon and daphne and sesame and miantanos, all the marvelous flavorings that we have used in our food for thousands of years. The men of Marathon carried small packets of these spices into battle, and the scents reminded them of their homes, their families, and their children."

He rose and tugged his napkin free from around his throat. "Cheese, you said. Cheese! Come closer, boy, and I will educate your abysmal ignorance." He motioned toward a wooden container on the counter. "That glistening white delight is feta, made from goat's milk, packed in wooden buckets to retain the flavor. Alexander the Great demanded it on his table with his casks of wine when he planned his campaigns."

He walked limping from the counter to the window where the piles of tomatoes, celery, and green peppers clustered. "I suppose all you see here are some random vegetables?" He did not wait for me to answer. "You are dumb again. These are some of the ingredients that go to make up a Greek salad. Do you know what a Greek salad really is? A meal in itself, an experience, an emotional involvement. It is created deftly and with grace. First, you place large lettuce leaves in a big, deep bowl." He spread his fingers and moved them slowly, carefully, as if he were arranging the leaves. "The remainder of the lettuce is shredded and piled in a small mound," he said. "Then comes celery, cucumbers, tomatoes sliced lengthwise, green peppers, origanon, green olives, feta, avocado, and anchovies. At the end you dress it with lemon, vinegar, and pure olive oil, glinting golden in the light."

He finished with a heartfelt sigh and for a moment closed his eyes. Then he opened one eye to mark me with a baleful intensity. "The story goes that Zeus himself created the recipe and assembled and mixed

59

the ingredients on Mount Olympus one night when he had invited some of the other gods to dinner."

He turned his back on me and walked slowly again across the store, dragging one foot slightly behind him. I looked uneasily at the clock, which showed that it was a few minutes past one. He turned quickly and startled me. "And everything else in here," he said loudly. "White beans, lentils, garlic, crisp bread, kokoretsi, meat balls, mussels and clams." He paused and drew a deep, long breath. "And the wine," he went on, "wine from Samos, Santorini, and Crete, retsina and mavrodaphne, a taste almost as old as water . . . and then the fragrant melons, the pastries, yellow diples and golden loukoumades, the honey custard galatobouriko. Everything a part of our history, as much a part as the exquisite sculpture in marble, the bearded warriors, Pan and the oracles at Delphi, and the nymphs dancing in the shadowed groves under Homer's glittering moon." He paused, out of breath again, and coughed harshly. "Do you understand now, boy?"

He watched my face for some response and then grunted. We stood silent for a moment until he cocked his head and stared at the clock. "It is time for you to leave," he motioned brusquely toward the door. "We are square now. Keep it that way."

I decided the old man was crazy and reached behind the counter for my jacket and cap and started for the door. He called me back. From a box he drew out several soft, yellow figs that he placed in a piece of paper. "A bonus because you worked well," he said. "Take them. When you taste them, maybe you will understand what I have been talking about."

I took the figs and he unlocked the door and I hurried from the store. I looked back once and saw him standing in the doorway, watching me, the swirling tendrils of food curling like mist about his head.

I ate the figs late that night. I forgot about them until I was in bed, and then I rose and took the package from my jacket. I nibbled at one, then ate them all. They broke apart between my teeth with a tangy nectar, a thick sweetness running like honey across my tongue and into the pockets of my cheeks. In the morning when I woke, I could still taste and inhale their fragrance.

I never again entered Barba Nikos's store. My spell of illness, which began some months later, lasted two years. When I returned to the streets I had forgotten the old man and the grocery. Shortly afterwards my family moved from the neighborhood.

Some twelve years later, after the war, I drove through the old neighborhood and passed the grocery. I stopped the car and for a moment stood before the store. The windows were stained with dust and grime, the interior bare and desolate, a store in a decrepit group of stores marked for razing so new structures could be built.

I have been in many Greek groceries since then and have often bought the feta and Kalamata olives. I have eaten countless Greek salads and have indeed found them a meal for the gods. On the holidays in our house, my wife and sons and I sit down to a dinner of steaming, buttered pilaf like my mother used to make and lemon-egg avgolemono and roast lamb richly seasoned with cloves of garlic. I drink the red and yellow wines, and for dessert I have come to relish the delicate pastries coated with honey and powdered sugar. Old Barba Nikos would have been pleased.

But I have never been able to recapture the halcyon flavor of those figs he gave me on that day so long ago, although I have bought figs many times. I have found them pleasant to my tongue, but there is something missing. And to this day I am not sure whether it was the figs or the vision and passion of the old grocer that coated the fruit so sweetly I can still recall their savor and fragrance after almost thirty years.

V

WE CALLED her Naka, the origin of that name lost somewhere in the garbled utterances of childhood. Her maiden name is lost, as well. She was of Swiss descent and had married a Greek-American named Joseph Angelos in Cairo, Egypt. He had been a chef in a resort hotel, and she tutored in French and German. When they returned to St. Louis, Missouri, they became active in my father's church and good friends of our family.

In later years Naka would speak proudly of having seen me at the hospital, on the night I was born, before my mother did. She had no children of her own by her marriage to Angelos, but they had adopted a boy who was about twelve the year I was born.

Late that year my family moved to Chicago. Shortly afterwards Joseph Angelos died of a stroke. Naka wrote my parents a desperate letter, telling them she had been left penniless, without a relative

63

to ask for help, asking if she could come with her son to stay with us for a while. My father warned my mother against the hazard and responsibility of taking another family into our house, but my mother's compassion won out. Naka arrived in Chicago a few days after receiving the letter from my mother. She remained with my family for twenty-five years.

In the beginning she came alone, her son remaining with friends in St. Louis. For a few months she slept on a pallet on the floor in the dining room because there wasn't a spare room or bed for her in our crowded house. When we moved in the spring to a larger apartment, there was an added bedroom for her. She wrote to St. Louis and her friends sent on to Chicago her son and her trunk.

I do not know what her son looked like when he first joined our family. By the time I was old enough to become aware of him, he had grown into a tall, slim, moody youth of nineteen or twenty, playing chess interminably with himself, while chewing relentlessly on the stem of a pipe.

The trunk I remember well as one of the marvels of my childhood. It was a cavernous metal receptacle, huge as the hold of a ship, the corners battered and dented, the surface smelling of oceans and distant cities, trussed with great strong belts and glistening buckles and lock. When it was placed in a corner of Naka's room, there wasn't enough space remaining to move freely from the dresser to the bed. But Naka vehemently rejected all suggestions that the trunk be emptied of its contents and stored in the basement. The trunk was her sturdy link to the past, an essential and integral part of her life. Within it were stored the memorabilia of her childhood and maidenhood, postcards, albums, diplomas, photographs, packages of faded letters tied carefully in ribbon, her wedding dress, pressed flowers from her bridal bouquet, a lace-edged handkerchief, a fluted fan. There were Easter and Christmas cards, mementos and souvenirs, trinkets and knickknacks, all things she treasured and touched with reverence, nostalgia, and affection. There was the leather-bound Bible her father had given her, the Bible she read each morning and each night. And there were the first picture-storybooks she had known as a child. As I grew old enough to understand the words and pictures, she drew these books from the trunk and read the stories to me.

In the shifting struggles going on between my mother and my father, Naka became my father's ally. She fashioned this alliance despite her awareness that my mother's compassion was the reason she lived in our house. But I think Naka could not help resenting my mother, envying her the sons and daughters born of her flesh and blood, a living husband, a house to manage, and a mission and position respected in the community.

By unwritten agreement Naka and my mother divided the household responsibilities. Naka prepared breakfast for the family, cooked the dinners my mother planned, with the exception of Sunday dinner, and ironed and washed our clothing. Since my mother was gone a good part of the day and evening, Naka's main responsibility was caring for my younger sister and me. She was attached to both of us, but she unfairly favored me. She protected me and spoiled me. On a very few occasions through my childhood she made a pretense of punishing me.

It is almost impossible for me after all these years to recall Naka as she was when I was a child. I can only remember her as she looked in the last ten years of her life. She had heavy, shapeless legs, discolored and distended by varicose veins. On one leg, torn in an auto accident years before, the knee was a mangled, scarred knob of flesh. She had gray hair that she wore short, thin lips that could curve into a lovely smile, and even white false teeth that added luster to the smile. She had a prominent mole on one cheek, and she wore metal-rimmed eyeglasses that etched two perpetual red marks across the bridge of her nose.

All I remember of her physical appearance was

related to age and decline, except for one memory, as a boy, when I saw her naked back, unblemished and curved with a strange seductive loveliness. That was only once, for most of the time she wore shapeless, sleeveless housedresses that she bought in Woolworth's for less than a dollar. With these housedresses she wore cheap cotton stockings that she tied into a knot below the knee, and felt house slippers. Pair after pair of these slippers always looked the same, whether they were new or worn, because as soon as she bought them she slit them at the toe and heel to relieve the pressure on her callused and corn-riddled feet.

In June of each year, as soon as school was over, one of my brothers would drive Naka, my sister, and me to a small cottage near a chain of lakes northwest of Chicago, where we spent the summer.

My father came out to stay with us whenever he could manage a day or two in the middle of the week. My mother rarely came to the cottage, because she accepted that abode as Naka's province. For two months out of each year Naka could be unquestioned mistress of a house, small and monastic as it was.

When I was about eleven, I was ordered to bed for a confinement that lasted almost two years. During my illness Naka cared for me with unflagging devotion and may well have saved my life.

After I had recovered, Naka sought to continue the same unyielding wardenship. We argued furiously over her efforts to choose my clothes, the meals I ate, the hours I came and went. If I stayed too late at a friend's house, Naka would phone the family and ask them to send me home. She was convinced that any girl who smiled at me was scheming to seduce me into a premature and illegitimate parenthood. When my patience had been driven to its limits, I reminded her ragingly that she was not my mother, that we were not bound by ties of blood, that she had no legitimate authority over my life. That merciless blow drove to the indefensible core of her grief. She would begin to cry and I, stricken by remorse, sought desperately to reassure her of my filial devotion. For days afterwards I accepted in expiation the full spray of Naka's maternal pollinations.

I consoled myself vengefully by asking Naka for money, knowing she would not refuse me. In the beginning, the amounts I requested were small, less than a dollar, but as I grew older and my activities expanded, I asked for several dollars at a time. She would complain querulously she did not have the money or that she needed it for certain small purchases of her own. When I persisted, she would go into her room and close the door. I'd hear her unlocking the trunk, unbuckling the belts, the creaking of the hinges as the lid was raised. A few moments later she would emerge from the room and silently, morosely, hand me the money I had asked for.

I came to marvel at the bottomless, never-ending cache of dollars in her trunk. I knew her only income, besides the few dollars my father gave her each week, was an old-age pension she had obtained a few years before, which provided her twenty-two dollars a month. Since my monthly requests easily equaled the combined amounts, I secretly believed she had inherited money from a legacy or an insurance policy, a bequest from her husband or a relative in Switzerland. As a consequence I paid little heed to her recurrent laments that she was virtually penniless.

In the last year of the war I married and left my father's house. By that time my sisters and brothers had already gone their separate ways. Naka's son had also married and moved to another city. Since my parents came home only to sleep, Naka spent her long days and a part of her nights alone. I knew she suffered loneliness, and I made resolutions to visit her regularly. But often weeks passed without my getting up to see her. I was working varied shifts at the steelmills, struggling to put the first trembling words from my heart on paper, trying to meet the whirling responsibilities of being a husband, and there was scant time remaining to consider Naka's distress.

I cannot recall the day or the week it was, nor even the season of the year (it might have been spring), nor the name of the horse I had been following that was scheduled to race at one of the tracks that afternoon. I had lost on him the last three times he had raced, and I was hungry to recoup. I had finished my shift at the mill, was broke (my usual condition), and decided to pass and see Naka for the first time in three weeks. I calculated an hour for the visit, ten minutes to get the loan, and I'd still reach the handbook in time for the race. With true fidelity to a sacred cause, I even planned to tell Naka I needed the ten dollars to purchase a toy I wanted for my newborn son.

When I arrived at my parents' building, I let myself in the lobby door with the key I still retained, and on the third floor inserted it into the lock of the door to the flat. The door opened only several inches before banging against the chain latched from inside. I shouted for Naka a few times, impatient at the unscheduled delay, but there wasn't any answer.

Thinking she might have gone down the back stairs and forgotten the chain on the front door, I went around through the yard and up the open stairs. The screen door of our flat was locked on the inside. I felt the first twinge of uneasiness and hurried around to the front door once more. After shouting and knocking loudly a few more times, I rammed my shoulder against the partly opened door, the weight of my body tearing the bracket of the chain loose from the wooden frame. I stepped inside and saw Naka lying on the floor in the hallway, still alive, but breathing harshly, her eyes staring at the ceiling as if she were blind.

Swept by panic and fear, I phoned for help. A few moments later a police ambulance arrived and the policemen came up with a stretcher. I rode with Naka in the ambulance to the hospital, where my father and mother joined me a short while later.

We kept a vigil at her bedside through the next two days. Still unconscious, she sucked breath hoarsely from the tubes of a tank of oxygen. I left the hospital from time to time, went home to my wife and son, returned to the hospital to sit beside her bed and wait. I cried a great deal during those two days, remembering all the years we had lived together, knowing that for better or worse she had helped form my own clay. I came to life in my mother's womb, but Naka's fierce love made for me a matrix of her own. For her devotion I gave a fragment of love, a little pleasure, but mostly ingratitude and abuse.

After a while I could not bear watching her fight for life any longer. I left to walk along the midway

71

near the hospital, and when I returned a couple of hours later, my mother waited for me outside Naka's room with tears in her eyes.

"Where have you been?" she asked.

"Walking," I said. "Is she dead?"

"She is dead," my mother said.

I have forgotten what Naka looked like in death, although I remember my father's dead face in that same hospital a few years later very well. It was as if death had effaced with a quick stiff brush what life had already blurred and muted. Naka died in the way she had lived, causing little change in the lives of those around her.

There was a funeral service for her in a Lutheran church, a spare, aseptic house of worship. There was a dark-cassocked, young and handsome minister in the pulpit, a cluster of our family, and a few friends among the pews. In deference to my father the minister delivered a short eulogy about a "woman he had never known, but a woman who had been, from all reports, good and true and faithful to her Christian trust and love."

We buried her in my father's plot, the first of the six family graves to be filled, her grave the one closest to the gravel road. Later, mostly because of my mother's urging and efforts, a small tablet of stone was placed at her head, recording simply her name, beneath it NAKA, and the dates of her birth and of her death.

A few days after the funeral, alone in my father's apartment, I sat in Naka's small bedroom. The room retained the thin musty scents of lavender water and sachet powder, and the pungence of the Mentholatum ointment she used for her arthritis. That was all that remained, besides her dresser, lamp, bed, Bible, and trunk.

In the small box on top of her dresser I found the key to her trunk and got down on my knees beside it. I wanted to separate the things I would keep and give to my sister and mother. But there was also a strange flutter of excitement in me, the feeling of an heir nearing the revelatory moment of his inheritance. I recalled the endless times over the years I had asked her for money and the way the trunk never failed my need. I unlocked the lock, unbuckled the straps, and raised the creaking lid.

When the last postcard, diploma, photograph, packages of faded letters tied carefully in ribbon, fan, lace-edged handkerchief, pressed flowers, memento and souvenir, trinket and knickknack she treasured had been spread upon the bed and the floor, I discovered her fortune, my inheritance, a total of eleven dollars stuck within the pages of an album that contained snapshots of me taken when I was a child.

So, I came finally to understand that the miracle of the trunk had not been money, but love, for which Naka hoarded her meager dollars, never failing the amount I asked for, and, in the end, leaving just enough reserve to settle the sum I wanted on the day I found her dying.

VI

THE COTTAGE where Naka, my sister, and I
spent the summers was frame-built, a single
large room partitioned into several smaller
rooms by thin plasterboard panels. As if it were some
lavish country house or manor, we painted the name
STELMARK in decorative black letters over the
front screen door. We formed this appellation by
joining the first syllable of my mother's name, Stella,
with my father's name, Mark.

The cottage stood on a dozen concrete posts (they
had been wooden posts until an onslaught of termites
required a recasting of the foundation). There was
no electricity or indoor plumbing, and water for
drinking and washing was obtained by violently flail-
ing a long-handled pump in the yard. Afterwards we
carried the filled buckets inside.

The trips we trudged to that small outdoor shack
made infamous in cartoon and story were always
traumatic. The odor was miasmic, there were webs
spun in the shadowed corners with spiders poised for

swift descent, while outside in the brush nameless creatures slithered through the weeds waiting for us to emerge. Sometimes, if a hornet or bee entered by way of the unscreened vents, we huddled in terror while the assassins droned ominously about our heads. These visits gained an added discomfort in September when the first chill of autumn came at twilight, and the wooden board with the cut-out seat was woefully cold.

But the summer days were long and golden and sometimes in the evening we sat on the porch with the kerosene lamps reflecting their quivering flames across the screens. Insects were drawn to the wire mesh, and large-winged dragonflies and moths beat vainly against the barrier. Outside in the darkness the crickets trilled their clamor, and in the distance on the stark, unplumaged branches of an old elm we called the "ghost-tree" an owl whooped its querulous cry.

The cottage was situated on a slight rise of hill above a pasture, woods around us, and a lake about a mile away. The hill was thick with trees—leafy maples, hardy oaks, and venerable catalpas and elms. Sometimes, in the frenzied winds that howled across the earth at night, the trees bent low, their branches scraping the roof and battering the eaves until it seemed the cottage would be crushed under their poundings. But we survived and in the morning the earth was cool, clean, and fresh, the trees purged of their weak boughs and frail leaves, the bushes and flowers glittering with drops of dew.

My father loved the cottage, the woods, and the lake. When he was able to escape his duties in the city, he'd catch a train late Wednesday or Thursday night to bring him into the depot of the small town, about six miles away, a little before midnight.

On the nights that we knew he was coming, my sister and I would lie awake in bed waiting for him. We fought sleep desperately until, just before midnight, we'd hear the clear, haunting wail of the train whistle as it passed Grant's Crossing before entering the town. We waited impatiently then, staring out the windows toward the pitch-black road. After about a half-hour we'd spot the lights of his taxi flaring across the upper foliage of the trees.

Naka, my sister, and I would hurry from our beds to wait for him at the door. There'd be a brief delay while he paid the driver, and then as the taxi backed and turned to leave, we'd see my father's tall figure striding through the yard. At the last moment, to discourage the mosquitoes, Naka would open the screen door with one hand and swipe at the air with the other. When my father entered, he kissed us, and I could smell the Aqua Velva lotion he used on his cheeks after shaving.

In the main room of the cottage that contained a

table and cots for my sister and me, we'd watch with delight as my father emptied his suitcase. There'd be a round loaf of church bread, fragrance of yeast and sanctity, a tall bottle of red wine, a box of candy, and fruit . . . fine oranges and pears and clusters of glistening dark grapes swollen with sweetness and juice.

"We will rise to go fishing at five," my father told me, and then he'd somberly ask. "How many worms?"

"A hundred," I answered. "Maybe more."

That was always an extravagant lie, which I justified by the knowledge that he rarely used more than fifty worms in a day's fishing. But he apparently endured nightmarish visions of being out in the middle of the lake, his boat anchored in a school of rampant fish, and discovering the big can of black earth devoid of any worms with which to bait his hook.

"Better dig some more in the morning," he said, because he understood my derelictions, and he'd kiss me goodnight. Naka went to her bedroom, and I'd slip into my cot on one side of the room, my sister already asleep in her cot on the opposite side.

My father entered the small bedroom, separated from our room by a drape, carrying the kerosene lamp. He'd put the lamp down on the small table and pull the drape across the doorway. Because the drape ended several inches from the floor, I followed the shadow of his movements as he undressed. Finally, I'd hear the springs in the mattress of the old metal-postered bed creaking as he slipped beneath the blanket. He'd read for a while, the newspaper rustling as he turned the pages. Then he'd lower the wick of the lamp and blow out the flame so the cottage sprang evenly into darkness. I'd finally turn to sleep, feeling the darkness warm and consoling because he was near.

It was still night when he shook me firmly awake. I'd stumble sleepily from bed, staring enviously at my undisturbed sister sleeping soundly. I'd wash, shivering, in cold water at the pump while Naka fried bacon and eggs. We'd eat breakfast on the porch as the first faint traces of dawn broke the rim of the night sky. Then, while my father assembled the gear, I'd unhappily dig out a dozen more worms. We started down the gravel road to the lake, laden with worm can, bucket for any fish we might catch, a Thermos of water, the oars for the boat, and the long bamboo fishing poles.

There were elegant homes astride the edge of the lake, green sloping lawns that swept down to the water, and whitewashed docks to which sleek motorboats were moored. The owners of those boats and their friends, I lamented to myself, did not have to trudge a mile loaded like mules with gear. They skimmed across the lake like gulls, and when they paused to fish, they cast with gleaming rods and reels, after selecting a fly from a colorful assortment of snares.

I stared longingly at the motorboats as my father and I launched the shabby little rowboat we kept tied to the residents' pier. While I sat in the stern, my father rowed us slowly to the center of the lake. The tranquil stillness of early morning hung across the water, and the shoreline around the lake was still cloaked in mist. The only sounds were the echo of our oars clumping in and out of the water, and perhaps a frog croaking on a lily pad, its mottled back awaiting the rising warmth of the sun.

Now and then my father paused, his forehead furrowed in concentration, until, as if he were suddenly in receipt of revelation from an unseen power, he'd boat his oars and wave his hand.

"Drop the anchor here," he said.

I'd peer skeptically over the side of the boat, seeing only the slimy tendrils of seaweed like wriggling serpents just beneath the surface of the water.

"Doesn't look to me like there's any fish here, Pa," I said.

"Here!" he spoke with conviction. "Right here!"

I'd lower the anchor and we'd unfurl the lines of the poles, bait our hooks with the worms, and then cast them into the water, where the tiny buoyant corks bobbed slowly in the slight ripples.

Sometimes we'd catch a few fish, small sunfish hardly the size of a man's hand, but my father pulled them in with the pride and delight of a man who had landed a marlin. He'd look at me with a gleam of triumph in his eyes as if his selection of place had been overwhelmingly vindicated. More often, however, we'd sit for hours without catching a fish, our corks and hooks undisturbed by the slightest nibble. And I'd become as desperate as a sailor, in the middle of an interminable voyage, for a return to port.

My father did not mind the hours of waiting. He sat slumped over his pole, humming under his breath, now and then brushing away a vagrant fly. I was awed and yet irritated, as well, at how much he seemed to enjoy doing nothing while I suffered. Once, only once, did the clamps of my patience shatter, and I cried out resentfully.

"What are you thinking of, Pa, sitting there for hour after hour, watching a cork that never moves?"

He raised his head and looked at me, suddenly understanding my impatience and distress. He nodded in a rueful apology and stared wistfully across the lake toward the pier where we tied our boat.

"I am thinking how quickly the time is passing," he said, "and how soon I must leave."

81

I never asked him again. After that day, by un-
spoken agreement, I stopped going fishing with him.
He'd rise before dawn and get ready to leave without waking me. He'd start down to the lake burdened with oars, buckets, and his poles. I was remorseful when I considered how much he enjoyed
having me with him, but I was grateful I did not
have to spend the endless, monotonous hours in the
boat. And by the time he returned in the late afternoon, only a few small fish in his bucket, he walked
with the vigor of a man who had spent a fruitful
day.

When the time came for him to return to the city,
my sister and I accompanied him in the taxi to the
town where he caught his train. Sometimes we ate
dinner together in one of the town restaurants, or
made a visit into the general store, where I replen-
ished the week's supply of pulp magazines. When
his train with the single coach pulled slowly puffing
into the station, we crossed with him to the depot.
He gave us each a quarter, paid the taxi driver to
drive us back home, and kissed us goodby.

He boarded the train and stood smiling down at
us from the top of the steps, tall and sturdy in his
black suit and white shirt and straw hat. He'd wave
to us and we'd run a short distance beside the slowly
moving train and stop as we reached the end of the
depot platform to shout a final goodby.

After my illness, when we stopped going to the cottage each summer, my father ceased going as well. He often made plans to spend a few days fishing there again. The plans never materialized. In the next few years he replaced the kerosene lamps at the cottage with electric lights, whether as an inducement for us or for himself I don't know. He visited the cottage once or twice more and then stopped pretending he was ever going again. There simply wasn't any pleasure for him in the empty rooms, eating alone, and going out to fish alone.

The cottage stood vacant for almost twelve years until my father's death. To the end he could not bring himself to sell the place, although he often needed the couple of thousand dollars the sale would have realized. But knowing he still owned the cottage provided him a consolation. After his death we sold it, and I do not remember mourning about its disposal.

Yet, when I look back from this vantage point in my life to the summers we spent in the cottage, I recall serene and contented hours lying beneath the crabapple tree, the sun speckling through the branches and leaves across my body. I remember standing beside the pump in the clear summer night, marveling at the chandelier of stars above my head. And I cannot hear the distant whistle of a train in the night without a tremor in my heart, re-membering the trains that brought my father to me.

Perhaps my homesickness comes because my fa-ther is dead and my youth has passed. I am ensnared in the details and rituals that burden us, the dilem-mas of work, family, society that we all yearn, at times, to flee.

Now, as my sons stir restlessly in my presence, impatient to return to their own pursuits, memories of the summers of long ago return. The words of a question I put to one of the boys are muted; instead I hear myself ask, "How many worms?"

The boy's lips move nimbly in answer, but instead of the tangled, evasive explanations about school, studies, or chores, I hear him respond.

"A hundred," he tells me. "Maybe more."

I am besieged then by a multitude of feelings . . . melancholia, amusement, awe at the way in which generations replay the endless games of the heart.

And I cannot help thinking how quickly the time is passing and how soon I will have to leave.

VII

MY ILLNESS came as quietly and unassumingly as twilight. A family friend, a doctor, was having dinner at our house one night, and my brother and sister teased me about being lazy. My mother mentioned my listlessness. An arrangement was made to phone the doctor for an appointment, and the following week Naka took me to his office.

He was a gentle and humorous man who prodded and tested me, bantering all the while to keep me at ease. In the course of an X-ray he discovered lesions on my lungs. The prescription was that I remain quietly in bed for a month.

My first reaction was pride at being able to return home to my brothers and sisters and boast of lesions, an ailment I did not fully comprehend but one sufficiently grave to require a month in bed. My second reaction, following quickly, was delight at the prospect of a month's vacation from school. I thought that a mistake had been made, that I couldn't feel as well as I did and be seriously ill. I even began to gloat that in some sly and canny way I had deceived the doctor, had pulled off a brilliant ruse.

Returning home from the doctor's office on that afternoon, I undressed and went cheerfully to bed thinking the whole affair a lark. I remained in bed, except for bimonthly visits to the doctor's office, for almost two years.

Those two years were a strange, intense period for me, weeks and months of boredom, excitement, discovery, despair, and terror. They affected my life, I am certain, more than any other interlude of my childhood and youth.

The small sun parlor in which I spent my days and nights was margined on three sides by rows of windows, and on the fourth side by two doors, one leading to the parlor and the other into the bedroom of my two older sisters. The room was just large enough for a bed, a couple of chairs, an end table, and a lamp.

Through the abundant encirclement of glass I watched and marked the coming and passing of the seasons. I went to bed in the autumn still indifferent to the gravity of my illness. Instead of rising hastily in the mornings as I had always done, I could idle the hours away, listening to the noises of activity in the house, until the last of my family, excepting Naka, were gone. I looked then toward the windows, enjoying the smells of the turning earth, the scent of burning leaves seeping into my nostrils. I felt like a warm, lethargic animal preparing to hibernate for the winter.

The birds assembled that autumn as they must have done every year, but I had never paid attention to them before. Now as one paused resting on the sill of my window, staring at me through the glass, I felt a latent kinship with them. Later, as the days grew shorter, I saw a flock of starlings, soaring and free, passing in synchronous flight over the roofs of the buildings across the street.

The autumn passed into the gray, bleak days of winter. Restless by then in bed, the cold wind pawing at my windows, the season reflected the desolation in my own body. Conscious of my illness for the first time, I lay for hours with my arms folded across my chest in a kind of senseless propitiation of the disease within me. Only when snow fell in the night, the first snow of winter, and I woke in the morning to see the fine flakes piled on my window sills, did I feel a redeeming in my heart. I rose from my bed and opened a window and dipped my fingers into the cold, moist snow, relishing the shivers that swept my body.

87

The spring came suddenly, abruptly, long after I'd given up hope that the relentless winter would ever end. It came in a bird's song, a strange, jubilant sound, because I had not heard a bird for months. Spring was evidenced, as well, in the tree across the street, a solitary maple dying year by year in the cincture of the arid city, yet still erupting a few buds on the branches that remained alive.

My mother brought me a small cluster of early-blooming April flowers, given to her from a neighbor's garden, and set them in a pitcher of water beside my bed. The scent of their blossoms rendered the air about me cloying and sweet, making me feel a disquieting nostalgia for something in the past to which I yearned to return.

The summer pounced like a cat, the terrible, scorching heat, discomfort, and sweat twisting sheets and pajamas about my body. The clamor of the city burst into my room through the open windows, trucks and horns and the cries of peddlers. Only in the occasional brief summer rain was there a momentary relief. The clouds that clustered to herald a storm, a rumble of thunder vibrating the frames of the windows, a sudden change in the wind. Naka hurried into my room to close and lock each window and draw the shades. I heard the first, heavy drops pelting the glass. And afterwards, I opened the windows to a fresh, clean, for a moment almost cool, scent of earth.

In the beginning of my confinement, to help pass the time, I read the pulp magazines I had been reading for years. The ones I loved best were those recounting the exploits of World War I flying aces. Eddie Rickenbacker, Frank Luke, the Red Baron (Charlie Brown has him now) the Lafayette Escadrille, the Spads, Sopwith Camels, DeHavillands, and Fokkers, all swooped and dived through my fantasies. I flew at the point of my squadron, a scarf billowing from my helmeted, goggled head. I dived endlessly, unfailingly, to the rescue of companions fighting off hordes of black-crossed Fokkers. These dogfights were always climaxed by my engaging the Fokker triplane of the Red Baron, a savage and brilliant duel between two masters, ending in a draw, so we could return to fight again. We dipped our wings to one another to acknowledge that we were foemen worthy of each other's skill. In the evening in the mess, we toasted our companions who had gone down in flames and drank and sang our heroic songs.

But in the middle hours of the dark and lonely night, when uneasiness and fear made me unable to sleep, I drew upon a swarm of heroes that belonged more distinctly to me. Achilles and Hector, Aga-

89

memnon and Odysseus entered my room carrying their great war swords. Brawny, bearded, and fearless men, they clustered about my bed, counseling and protecting me, hardening my resolve to grow well and strong so I might join them in the storming of enemy citadels.

As the months passed I moved from the sky above Flanders and from the battlements of Troy into a carnivorous assault upon a tattered set of the *Book of Knowledge* that we had in our house. Without program or direction I informed myself about the Suez Canal, Byzantium, Siam, the effect of the moon on the tides, the Sistine Chapel, the Pre-Cambrian period, Rembrandt, the Charge of the Light Brigade, Ode on a Grecian Urn, Why Grass Is Green, Mars and Venus, Merlin and Excalibur, Troilus and Cressida . . .

From the *Book of Knowledge,* which I finished completely in less than two months, stirred by the phantasmagorias of fiction, I moved to novels. My brothers and sisters began buying them for me in used-book stores or bringing them home from libraries. Quickly bored by the colonic Hardy boys and the humbug of Tom Swift, I began and discovered Irving, Hawthorne, Poe, Melville, Balzac, Maupassant. Gorki and Chekhov moved me to tears. But of all the books I read in this period, the one that touched me the most was *Martin Eden* by Jack Lon-

don. I identified my own hunger for knowledge with
Martin Eden's hunger, the obstacle of his ignorance
equated by the obstacle of my illness, both impediments to be overcome. In the end, even while savoring his triumph, I felt the chilling and indefinable
truth of his disillusionment and death.

During those interludes when my weary brain and
aching eyes prevented my reading, I lay motionless
in the bed listening to the sounds of the street. The
stillness in the morning after the children were in
school, a stillness broken only by the shrill squeaking
of a housewife's cart, now and then the petulant
voice of one of the women arguing with a janitor
about garbage or heat.

The hardest parts of the day for me to endure
were the afternoons when the children returned from
school and invaded the street beneath my windows.
I'd listen to their delighted shrieks as they played
baseball and tag, kick-the-can and hide-and-go-seek.
Their play lasted until twilight, when their mothers
called them in for supper, and only a few stragglers
remained calling to one another longingly across the
shadows.

Late at night, the streets quiet once more, I studied the reflections of the headlights of passing cars
flashing across my ceiling. When the street grew still
again, I'd listen intently for the sound of footsteps
on the pavements. It was easy to distinguish the hard,

heavy tread of a man opposed to the staccato tapping of a woman's heels. I listened to their footsteps coming nearer, for an instant rapping directly beneath my windows, and afterwards receding until the faint, final echoes merged into the murmurs of the city night.

I am not sure of just how it began, perhaps an erotic dream that caused a startling ejaculation, but in this period of visions and daydreams I discovered the sizzling pleasure that could be derived from rubbing the erogenous zones of my body. These new sensations, conveniently suited to pajamas and bed, delighted me, and I practiced them with ardor and zeal.

Most of the time I indulged myself when I was alone, but as a variant excitement, I became adept at masturbating in the presence of others, one hand concealed beneath my sheets, the other hand holding a book or magazine, strategically placed, to cover my throbbing erection. I took lightning-like advantage of any opportunity. When the twelve-year-old girl who lived upstairs came down to visit me, she leaned out my window to call to a friend in the street below, her dress hiking up her slender, glistening bare legs. I leaped to my quarry and in the space of time it took her to call out several words, close the window, and turn around, I had achieved my fevered release.

When there were no nubile young girls leaning out my windows, I utilized photos of girls in bathing suits from magazines, or the sleek, lovely girls in the underwear ads of the Sears Roebuck catalogues. Somehow none of these visual aids motivated my libido as effectively as words. Words were the prongs to skewer my excitement for the real feast. I remember a phrase from a story in one of the racier pulp magazines, a phrase I whispered as I masturbated.

"Relentless he thrust his rod between her golden thighs . . ."

I used pictures, images and fantasies, and once, God help me, barely avoiding what might have been permanent injury, the wrapped beaters of a Mixmaster, but none of these artifacts could match the ardor of those words:

"Relentless he thrust his rod between her golden thighs . . ."

Yet, ancient as the story of Creation and the aborted sojourn in Eden, my innocence and joy were darkened by the knowledge that I had sinned, and kept sinning. The serpents of guilt and remorse joined me in my moist bed. I anticipated in terror the consequences of my aberration—blindness, madness, the rotting and withering away of my limbs.

A more severe crisis of illness lay ahead of me, and my terror aggravated the condition. One night I coughed up specks of blood, and the doctor came grim and foreboding. After he had examined me I heard him gravely discussing with my parents the possibility of sending me to a sanitarium.

I became reluctant to sleep, in fear that death would come and snatch me away. I fought sleep, and when my burdened eyes finally closed and I dozed, demons and wild-beaked monsters ripped and dismembered my body. I woke screaming and did not dare close my eyes again. Sometimes my mother sat with me, or one of my brothers and sisters, but mostly the task fell to Naka. She sat for hours in a chair beside my bed while I watched tensely so that she did not leave me alone.

On those nights I slept fitfully for a few hours and woke in the darkness, the rooms about me silent as a grave, I'd hurry from bed and go to one of the bathrooms and lock the door to wait out the night. As a result of these excursions I first began to play the role of voyeur.

The bathroom was narrow, with a single frosted window facing the window of a furnished house-keeping room across the gangway. By sitting on the rim of the tub in the dark bathroom and opening our window an inch, I could peer directly into the room across the way, see the small icebox, stove, table, chairs, and foot of the bed.

Three different tenants occupied that room over the following four to five months. The first one was a woman, possibly around fifty, who came home at the same time each evening. She changed into a silk Chinese dressing gown adorned with dragons and scrolls. She turned on the radio, fixed her dinner, and sat down to eat it alone. After dinner she'd wash the few dishes, read a newspaper or a magazine, and then polish her nails. Finally, she'd brush her hair, leave the room to go to the bathroom next door, and return to go to bed.

Her routine resembled a familiar film running over and over. Whenever I began to watch, I knew what had gone before and what would follow. Her rituals were solitary and identical. I never saw another man or woman with her in the room.

In the beginning I watched her, titillated at the prospect of seeing her undress. After a while I watched in wonder, marveling at the weary, unchanging tedium of her routine. And then, one night, I saw her put down the emery board with which she was smoothing her nails. For a moment she sat rigid, and then she put her head down into her hands. After an instant I understood she was crying, a silent, desperate unleashing of tears. I felt witness to some revelation of loneliness and grief that belonged in the domain of God. I fled the bathroom, and for a while I dared not look across the gangway.

That was in the early spring. One night a few weeks later when I entered the bathroom, the window open several inches, I saw the light of the window across the way and heard the sound of husky, male laughter. Apprehensive but curious as to whether the woman had found a friend, I went to peer through the narrow opening.

There was a strange woman in the room. She wore a slip, was lean and dark with a coarse, unlovely face. The man who had laughed was bald-headed, with beefy, hairy arms, wearing underwear shorts and top. At that moment he grabbed the woman, pulling her hard against him, clawing at her breasts, dragging her toward the bed. They fell across the bed, and although I could not see their sexual union, the foot of the mattress rocked violently.

Each night after that, he had another woman. Sometimes one looked familiar, but for the most part they resembled one another in being hard-featured, misshapen, with sagging, blemished breasts. They were graceless and unredeemed for me by any vestige of beauty. Yet the bald-headed man embraced them and dragged them to his bed. After the union,

96

he swaggered and strutted naked around the room, his belly hanging, and what seemed to me to be a huge penis and testicles dangling in a clump of dark tangled hair. In a little while he'd make a motion with his organ toward the woman, a gross gesture that appeared to excite her and delight him. Then he'd be on her again like an animal seeking something to ravage and tear apart.

I wondered many absurd and terrible things, if that confrontation between man and woman comprised the romantic world of adult love I had read about in poetry and novels. Were all the words merely a mask for that graceless assault of bodies, that savage tearing of flesh against flesh?

Then the big-cocked, bald-headed devourer of hideous women moved away. A young couple rented the room. The girl was blonde, with silky, glistening hair and a radiant face. The man was handsome and vigorous. They pranced and played together as if they were children, smacking and pinching, teasing and giggling, laughing and shrieking. Sitting across from one another at the small table, eating their dinner, he might jump up and take her into his arms for a buoyant little dance. And one twilight when she was alone, waiting for him, I saw her sweeping the room, completely naked. She sang softly as she swept, her bare feet gliding across the floor in a kind

97

of lithe, glowing grace, her exquisite golden-nippled breasts trembling in the enchantment of her joy.

Strangely, then I grew better, the lesions healing, my confinement drawing to an end. I know that my recuperation did not come about for any reason except the long months in bed. Yet, over the years that have passed since then, I have also come to accept and believe in the therapeutic benefits I received from the young couple across the way.

They were young and, I think, poor, their housing confined to a single wretched room, but they radiated love and joy in being alive. The light of their happiness filtered even into the dark, guilt-riddled world of my nightmares and terrors. And I believe with all my heart that they strengthened my bond to life and my desire to live.

VIII

WHEN I emerged from the bilious and morose solitude of my two years' illness, I fell like a newborn babe into a startling world. The tranquil mornings, lingering afternoons, evenings creeping from twilight into darkness, were blown apart by the smacking winds of scramble and haste.

Naka woke me at dawn. I hurried to dress, gulped a few swallows of milk, chewed a piece of toast, rushed to school, moved rapidly from class to class. Lunchtime in the midst of hundreds of boys and girls passed with bewildering swiftness. The afternoon vanished into dinner and the homework to be done until bedtime. Although my years of reading had made me proficient in words and stories, I had fallen behind in science and mathematics. I had to work furiously merely not to fall further behind.

I was once again conscripted into household service, no longer spared my share of family tasks, or running errands to the store. Before I knew it the time had come for me to fall wearily into bed and after some hours of sleep rise for another belabored day. Time, so long an indolent friend, became a relentless taskmaster.

Adding to my confusion was the detonating nearness of all the lovely girls I had only dreamed and schemed about during the past two years. Upon the barren soil of my graceless reentry into the world burst all the seedlings of girlhood, shrill, shrieking hordes of peahens, ewes, does, and tigresses.

I moved precariously between high little breasts, round undulating bottoms, and bare glistening legs, stammering and mumbling, faltering and longing. In a group of students walking up the stairs I stumbled a number of times when the golden legs of girls flashing above me caused me to ignore my own gait.

I was racked by formless agonies, loving first one beauty and then another, bestially desiring all, tormented lest my lust be revealed in scarlet letters on my face.

At fourteen I had grown taller and stronger, but also more ungainly and awkward. My ears, which had always been long-lobed, hung like the appendages of a retriever from my lopsided head. The constant reading during my illness had strained my eyes and I wore metal-rimmed eyeglasses (how fashionable they are now) that rested on the bridge of my substantial nose giving me the brooding appearance

100

of a myopic hawk. I was hardly concocted to bring a flutter to any young girl's heart, but that did not keep me from loving them.

By the time I was fifteen I had mustered enough tatters of confidence to ask a few girls out. Our dates were generally hand-holding marathons along the lake or in the park, Coke and sandwich excursions into a sweetshop, sometimes—dependent upon my tenuous finances—even a movie.

I began to write love lyrics, sad, melancholy hymns of unrequited desire. A girl praised my voice, and in a delirium of delight I composed and sang a song for her in the basement of her building while a crowd of scoffers hooted and howled in the backyard. I wrote another poem about the lovely teen-age daughter of a neighborhood butcher and sent it to her house via Special Delivery mail. The butcher intercepted my ode, opened the letter (violating the privacy of the U.S. mails) and carried it angrily to my father for translation. My father pondered the poem a few moments and then explained courteously to the butcher that it was not written in Greek.

My father warned me gently of misusing the mails, and the butcher, wary of the syntax of my passion, banished me from crossing the steps of his porch forever. Remembering the dismembered sides of beef that hung in his icebox, I religiously obeyed. If my darling had been a princess waiting for me to rescue her from the tower of the evil butcher's castle, she must be languishing there yet.

There was a girl named Betty with a sweet and tuneful laugh, a girl named Greta with hair the citreous shade of the honey that my mother used to gild her pastries, and a girl named Irma with a shapely contrapuntal behind that bedazzled the eyes. Once, from a window of our third-floor apartment, seeing her passing on the street below, I leaned out so far I knocked off the screen and nearly fell out myself.

For a few fervid weeks I was enamored of a black-eyed girlfriend of my sisters who visited often in our house. I admired the reckless and insouciant way she lounged upon the floor, her skirt up almost to her waist, exposing a stunning acreage of leg and thigh. She walked in on me once while I was sitting on the stool in the bathroom, my trousers crumpled around my ankles, and I avoided her after that. Good breeding suggested a knock on the closed door first, and there are certain events even love may not survive.

I was sixteen, nearly seventeen by then, a somber and serious youth, withdrawn and grave as a pall-bearer, with a pedant's vocabulary and a face that considered it an affliction to laugh.

The panzers of Adolph Hitler had just invaded Poland, and there was little reason for a young man approaching draft age to laugh, anyway. In sudden rejection of brainless, insipid girls I directed my libidinal arrows toward a teacher of twenty-five who consented to picnic and play tennis with me a few times. We spent some lovely afternoons on the grassy banks of the lagoon in Jackson Park while I read her the poetry of Swinburne and Yeats. When I grew more serious and ardent about her, she gently disengaged herself. Her affection seemed genuine and her remorse at our separation unrehearsed. That consoled me even as I sorely missed the hours we had spent together.

There were a few other girls during my first years in high school, a random assemblage of dates, some improvident fumbling on shadowed park benches, and then there was Marina.

She was about five years older than my seventeen, a junior at the University of Chicago while I was a junior in high school. We met at a gathering of our families, related to one another through my sister's marriage to a relative of Marina's. She was an attractive, articulate girl with exquisite almond-shaped eyes and comely full lips. She was pensive and serious with a quality of melancholy that drew me to her.

I did not have the courage in the beginning to ask her to go out with me. Instead, when I got out of school in the afternoon, I hurried to the University library where she studied and sat at an empty

103

desk close to her. I studied myself, sometimes, since it was the supposed reason for my presence. Much more often I spent the time watching the radiance of her face as she pondered over a book. I came to know each small gesture of her hands, the way she tapped her pen impatiently at a page whose thesis displeased her, or the way she flung back the strands of taffy-colored hair that fell forward across her cheek. Sometimes she'd look up and catch me watching her. She'd shake her head reprovingly and motion me back to my books. Then, relenting, she would console me with a warming little smile.

Afterwards we walked in the twilight across the campus arguing heatedly about books. She often humiliated me by exposing my intellectual inconsistencies and pretensions. I felt like a scolded child even as I was forced to accept the truth of her observations. Still, there were a few times she was moved to admit she gained some insight from me, an emotional intuition her severe rationalism prevented her comprehending.

We walked to the Illinois Central train station that ran trains to the far southern city suburb in which she lived. I waited on the platform with her until the train arrived. After she boarded the train, for a final, fleeting moment I'd catch a glimpse of her arm raised in a brief farewell through the glass of the door. Then she would be lost to me in a surging blur of train windows. I would stand on the platform staring wistfully after the train until the two small red lights on the rear of the last car were lost in the darkness.

For several months we spent afternoons like that, studying, walking, and talking. All that time I never even dared take her hand. There was a wariness and dignity about Marina that discouraged any liberties. In addition, there was the difference in our ages. This fact bothered her a great deal, and she berated herself for keeping me from girls my own age, ignoring my protests that I couldn't stand the silly adolescents. The difference in our ages also caused her to become, at times, insufferably maternal, advising and admonishing me on matters of growing up until my teeth were set on edge.

I tried desperately to grow up as fast as I could. I shaved twice a day to stimulate the growth of my beard and brushed my hair in various ways to appear older. I practiced before the mirror with a pipe in imitation of the suave Ronald Colman. I even bought a pair of elevator lifts to wear in my shoes so I might stand taller beside her. She discovered the deception when we sat together on the grass and she noticed my heels rising out of my shoes. She did not mock or laugh at me, but gently consoled my distress by reassuring me that I was older than my years.

When our families discovered the amount of time we were spending together, they became fearful. Marina had to finish college, and I was still in high school. The pressures made her peevish, and she suggested we stop seeing one another for a while. I argued bitterly with her but she firmly prevailed.

We did not see each other for several months after that. I missed her poignantly, but pride prevented my telephoning her or making an effort to see her against her wishes. I passed a desolate and lonely summer.

One night, in the beginning of September, Marina telephoned me at home and asked if I could meet her on campus. I was surprised and grateful and I hurried to the Midway. We walked for hours on that night and for the first time I sensed the violent confusions and uncertainties that beset her, the people and events she felt helpless to control. Convinced that her destiny would be a significant one, she still possessed a strong apprehension that her capacities were limited, her talents frail. The brutal war that was killing young men her own age demanded she take a part, fashion a contribution that would help toward peace. Yet she lacked any sense of the direction these efforts should take. Above all else she felt the haunting mystery of life, the predicament between having been made in God's image, and the

106

incrimination of being descended from fallen Adam.

We walked from the park to the edge of the lake, sitting on the ledge of rocks along the water. South of us the red flaring flames of the mills reflected into a sky that she said made her think of the burning of a bombed city in Europe. We sat huddled close together, our fingers tightly clasped.

Swept by the memory of the misery and loneliness I had felt during the months of our separation, I confessed to Marina that I loved her, poured out to her the brimming fullness of my heart. For the first time, that night we kissed.

I wonder now if time has not ornamented that kiss, if the years have not made of the memory more than it was. Yet, I remember, too, a strange intense bonding of our hearts, a union of spirits under the burning sky, and the sadness of the passing summer. And I understand now her terror, as well. Because even then she must have felt herself drifting, slipping away from the moorings that held her to life.

She could not tell me she loved me because it would not have been true. She told me she cared for me very much, had missed me, too, wanted us to remain close together. Perhaps time would provide us an answer.

For a few weeks after that night I journeyed exultantly to the library once again. We walked on campus as we had done months before. There was, for the first time, a greater measure of equality between us, the distress because of the difference in our ages muted and diffused by her fear and need. For the first time, as well, I took a train to the suburb where she lived and we spent the day together, walking, talking, visiting with her family. Her father was a steelworker, a good and taciturn man. Her mother was a quiet, kind, and somber woman. Neither of them, like so many immigrant parents, was able to understand their daughter, born and reared in the new land.

There was an afternoon at the beginning of October. I went to meet Marina at the library, carrying a small tissue-wrapped cluster of violets I had bought from a flower vendor on the street. She told me gravely she wanted to talk to me, and we sat in a deserted corner of the library. She told me we could not see one another again. She liked me, enjoyed being with me, but neither of these compensated for the guilt she felt because of my age, her fear that she was distracting me from my studies. She advised me to forget her, concentrate on my studies, develop my talents as a writer or as a priest.

I grew angry, called her fickle and a fool, accused her of caring for someone else. I threw the violets bitterly at her feet and left.

Almost a year passed before I saw Marina again. It was at the end of the summer of 1941. She had graduated from the University in June and had enrolled for graduate study beginning in the fall. I was eighteen, had finished high school, and had just registered for the draft.

We met one afternoon by chance at my sister's house, and I walked Marina to the train she was taking home. She appeared lovelier to me than ever before, endowed with the same fragile grace I remembered. But there was a further change in her, a curious sadness and withdrawal, a quiet resignation that permeated her words and feelings. All the agitation and distress she had revealed the year before, about her life and the war, was gone, leavened into a passive and unconcerned calm.

The year's separation had cooled some of my ardor and my bitterness. I was pleased when she said I seemed older, more mature. We talked quietly of a few books and of remaining good friends always.

We walked up the steps to the station platform, and a moment later the train pulled in, stopped, and the doors slid open. Marina boarded one of the cars and turned as she had done so many times on those nights we walked from the library and waved a fleeting farewell to me through the glass of the door. Even that gesture seemed somehow changed, an action performed by memory without significance or purpose. Yet I had no sense of foreboding, nothing beyond a feeling of strangeness about her.

A few weeks later Marina killed herself. She took a gun her father kept in their house as a precaution against thieves and put the gun to her heart and pulled the trigger. She died without leaving a note or speaking a final word to anyone.

There have been many times over the years since then when I have felt Marina's destiny was decided, her death foreshadowed when she first opened her eyes to life. It is a lighter burden to carry than to consider that if I had been older, less filled with the vanity and passion of my youth, I might have comprehended her terror, the spindles of the loom on which she wove her decision to die. I don't know. I have learned since then that we can live beside those we love and not really discern the measure of their longings and their loneliness. In the midst of multitudes we exist like barricaded islands, fearful or unwilling to reveal ourselves or to discover the meaning of others. Even had I loved Marina more, I am not sure I could have held her to a life she no longer desired to live.

I know that within my stories, the fragments of her that I loved will forever endure even as they wear the masks of other faces and speak words from other mouths. For she has left within me, as long as

I live, the image of a fragile and melancholy spirit who died in her blooming twenty-fourth year because her soul, like that of a wild bird, could no longer endure the cages of man and the caverns of earth.

IX

THE FIRST exposure I had to gambling came when I entered a bookie's with a friend who had come to collect on a bet. I looked around with wonder and amusement at the large room crowded with men and women, faces raw and stark with excitement and longing.

I returned alone after a few days, as much to observe as to bet. Little by little I began arriving earlier, making a few small bets on various races, and staying around to see how they fared. I started cutting one class at school and then two and three. After about a month, the static, monotonous routine of school could not equal the ebullient curriculum of the races, and I stopped going to class completely. I deceived my parents and Naka by leaving for school in the morning at my usual time. I'd walk down to the bookie behind the Illinois Central station on 63rd Street, under the tangled arabesque of the elevated tracks. I'd pass the scrutiny of a hooligan at the door and then walk up a dimly lit flight of stairs to enter a large, unadorned, and brightly illuminated room.

At that time of morning, before any of the day's races had begun, the room would be sparsely occupied. Aside from the cluster of employees preparing for the day's activity, there were a few early arrivals like myself, earnestly studying the long sheets tacked to the walls that listed the horses running at tracks across the country.

I'd find a chair along the wall and spread my scratch sheet and Racing Form across my knees. I'd diligently ponder the past performances of the horses running that day, their assigned weights, the jockeys riding them, the distances they would run. Each time I raised my head there would be a few more people in the room, a rising mutter of voices, a musty odor of shabby, worn clothing.

When the wire service announcer came on at eleven o'clock to record the first changes in the line posted the night before, the room was about half-full, suffused with cheerfulness and buoyant spirits. Men and women called gaily to one another, their voices sparked by anticipation. The disruptive defeats of the day before had been forgotten in the luminous dawning of a new day.

By noon the room was rumbling and crowded. There were grillmen from nearby lunchrooms, gravy and soup stains like badges on their soiled jackets;

113

waiters who wouldn't start serving food until later in the day; ebony-faced redcaps from the railroad station; housewives with grocery money clutched tightly in their fingers; girls with bleached hair and rouged cheeks looking as if they had bounced all night and were exhausted; pensioners, sports, shopkeepers, the dispossessed and the unemployed, fleeing flophouse cot and soup kitchen coffee and roll, and pimpled, jittery youths with the first fuzz of beards sprouting on their pale cheeks.

As post time neared at the first of the tracks to begin racing, I'd rise and merge with the crowd, joining its fetid and yet compelling affability. We shoved in ragged, amiable lines toward the impassive ticket-writers sitting in a row behind the long table. After getting down our bets we'd straggle to form a tight, worshipful cluster of bodies and pale, vigilant faces beneath the loudspeaker. We'd stare up at the disk of wire netting as if it were a venerable idol from which we might conjure, by sheer force of our faith and longing, the benediction we yearned to hear.

When the loudspeaker cried, *"They're off!"* we answered with a constricted and explosive gasp followed by silence. With each call we swayed, prayed, groaned, or cursed. Some could not remain rooted in one place and shuffled like graceless dancers within the tight circles of space in which each of us was confined. As the horses entered the stretch, a fervent murmuring of hope and despair began, fading into the most unremittingly tense silence I have ever known. When the godhead announced its final verdict, we answered with a roar.

If we had won, we'd wave our tickets over our heads, informing all the others that we had triumphed, that sagacity and virtue had been rewarded. We'd push jubilantly toward the small line forming before the cashier, our tongues loose in the babble of gleeful children.

When we lost, we'd throw our tickets fitfully away, twisting in frustration because we had ignored all the pertinent data that pointed to the obvious winner. With each defeat we'd struggle harder to salvage the glow of our early ardor.

But we were given scant time to mourn or cheer. Other tracks began their races, the loudspeaker droning steadily of last-minute changes in odds, weights, and jockeys, horses at the post, races beginning. We rushed to place bets before the first call shut us out, waited, listened, whirled like dervishes before the confusion of several races starting at the same time.

And through the hours of the day, our pores exuded bile and sweat, hope and fear. Our cramped bowels hissed, a burning in our kidneys erupted sometimes out of control. But we accepted these debilities in others and in ourselves without disgust or reproach. We understood that the canonized purgings of these poisons evoked a catharsis that would leave us clean and guiltless once again.

By late afternoon only the final races at a few of the tracks remained to be run. The crowd was small again, the ones who had gone broke driven out. A few winners, very few, quitting while they were still ahead. Other winners still played, casual and loose in their victory. The losers with a little money left played desperately in the final hours to redeem the day. For until the very end, until the last horse had run the last course, a dream of tagging a longshot on which to finish triumphant was always possible.

When the loudspeaker had finally gone mute, those of us who still remained stood uncertainly in the large, nearly deserted room, our feet treading the carpet of shredded, discarded tickets that littered the floor. Finally, slowly and reluctantly, we'd move toward the door, looking back one final wistful moment at the room darkening under silence and shadows.

Often, unwilling to relinquish the warm bonds of the day, we'd gather in bars and restaurants along the street, recounting endlessly to whoever would listen how narrowly victory had evaded us. A photo finish, the blocking or bumping of our horse around a turn, a jockey's poor ride, these were the broken records of our lament. On and on we performed our indignant autopsies until it was time to go out to the newsstand and meet the evening delivery of the Racing Form with the index and past performances of the horses running the following day.

Sometimes, pondering those capricious days I remember old Gero Kambana. He was a white-haired old man with turbid and creviced cheeks dark as the bark of an ancient tree. For seventy-five of his ninety years on earth, he had been abstemious in all facets of his life but gambling. He had never married, never given any woman more than the embers from the fire of his true love. When I met him for the first time, he was almost blind and nearly deaf. But he sat for hours in a corner of the gambling room, absorbing the tension and excitement, now and then crying out at something he imagined he saw or heard.

I would place a bet for him and return to sit beside him while the race was run. He would stare from his bright almost sightless eyes at the sheets where the marker chalked the changes in odds, his ears pendent toward the loudspeaker over which the wire service announcer made his calls. All through the race, unable to distinguish the name of one horse from another, Gero Kambana sat trembling in his chair, his cheeks shaken in suspense. At the finish of the race I'd tug at his sleeve and make a sign close

117

to his eyes letting him know whether he had won or lost. He hissed exultantly when he won and grunted a curse when he lost. I came to understand he didn't really care. The old man lived only for the ritual of suspense, the frenzy of gambling. The mystery was not in the beginning or in the end, but in the moment of play.

Was there ever a time, I have often wondered, when the old man could still have made a choice about his life? At what point were the patterns of his days and his nights set unalterably?

For a while I was certain that unlike Gero Kambana I could cease gambling whenever I wished. That facile boast reassured me even though the hours I wasn't gambling hung over me like a pall. I'd wake at night yearning for daylight. If I could not fall asleep again, I'd rise and study the Racing Form, trying to elicit shamanic vibrations as I murmured the names of different horses. Now and then, with a premonitory uneasiness, I swore if I made a killing, I'd quit gambling. I did not realize how ancient and benighted an oath that was.

Since I lost more often than I won, money to play with remained an incessant problem. I wheedled a few dollars at a time from Naka, made out false receipts for items supposedly purchased for school which I gave to my father, explaining that I had borrowed the money from a friend. I begged money from relatives and friends without the slightest comprehension how I would repay them. I sold my books and the books I borrowed from others. (The *Dialogues* of Plato was lost on a maiden named Marty's Choice, and Oswald Spengler's *Decline of the West* was lost on a filly named Carmela.)

Every item and artifact in our house I recurrently appraised in terms of the amount of money it might bring. Once I even sold a suit belonging to one of my brothers and suffered a stricken remorse as he searched desperately to find it. In this untamed period I came to understand the brutal dimensions of my obsession.

I had been dating Diana, a girl I had known from childhood, for a year and half. Soon after the war we decided to marry. She knew of my gambling, but we were both convinced of the reforming zeal of love, anticipating that marital responsibility might be the raft on which I'd flee the whirlpool.

We rented a third-floor kitchenette apartment that had three windows looking out on a huge shadowed court of similar apartments. Diana found a job as a salesgirl in a downtown department store. I had an evening job in a neighborhood liquor store. We decided I'd look for full-time employment and meanwhile could spend my days reading and writing.

Following this program, we rose early in the morning and had breakfast together, and then I'd walk Diana to the 47th Street station where she'd catch the train going downtown. After leaving her I'd walk on to the Blackstone Library, a high-ceilinged and cavernous building. I'd locate a table in a corner of one of the reading rooms and assemble my books, pencils, and pads.

For a little while, in a flurry of eagerness, I read and made copious notes. An hour would pass swiftly. After it seemed to me I had been working through lunch, I'd catch a glimpse of the clock on the wall and be surprised to find it was only eleven o'clock. My attention began wandering. When I sought to concentrate, the words in the book blurred slightly before my eyes. I envisioned the gambling room, the early patrons and my cronies preparing for the zestful day. The first New York track began racing at about one o'clock and as the time dragged interminably toward that hour, I grew more restless. I pushed aside my books and leafed through a series of magazines and newspapers hoping they'd provide a halter for harnessing my interest. But in the oppressive silence of the library, a librarian's cough erupting like a minor explosion, I couldn't evade the ticking of the clock that swept like wind into the remotest corners of every room. I felt a constricting in my chest, a mounting panic that if I did not flee the library, I would somehow cease to breathe.

The first time I abandoned the library, the first of what would be countless times, I hurried along the street with my head down, guilt and shame burning my body. But when I entered that great, warm womb and lost myself within the tribe, my grief was aborted and spirit and joy merged once more in my heart.

The following year a good friend of mine and I purchased a small, dingy lunchroom in a factory and railroad district. As my share of the down payment I used the $1200 my wife had saved in three years of working before our marriage. In some cave of the winds I had heard that all any Greek (even one born in America) needed to grow wealthy in a restaurant was to possess a facility for rapidly opening and closing a cash register. After about a month, the long, tedious hours of labor an abrasive prison, I relinquished that sacrosanct mirage.

My parole began when I discovered a bookie operating in the railroad yards a few blocks away, his base of operations a small, shabby carpenter's shanty with hand-scrawled placards warning patrons not to urinate in the corners. Five or six times a day I'd slip down to the shanty to make a few bets and check the outcome of the earlier races.

The man who had sold us the lunchroom had been in the restaurant business for thirty years. My friend

121

and I could not match his canny experience in buying or in salvaging the scraps. When we began to lose money each week, the long hours we were forced to work became unbearable. We decided one man should remain to salvage, if possible, the floundering wreck. We flipped a coin and I lost.

I managed to hang on a few precarious months by firing the cook and waitress and taking over their duties myself. I still retained a dishwasher, and when I wanted a fast jaunt to the bookie's shanty, easing my despair in the fashioning of parlays and daily doubles, I left him in charge of the lunchroom, an assignment hardly calculated to improve my business.

In the early autumn of that year we discovered my wife was pregnant. She worked a few more weeks and then had to stop. Without her salary to aid us in meeting our expenses, we edged closer to calamity. The crisis came in the first week of November when I lacked the money for the rent on my apartment and for the payment of the mortgage on the lunchroom.

On a few occasions in the past, to pay an overdue gas or electric bill, I had borrowed small sums of money from my father, money I knew he wasn't really able to afford. Since there was no place else to turn, I went to him again in November. Diana looked after the lunchroom while I rode a bus to my father's church. In his office, subduing my shame, I asked him for $150. That was a huge amount for him then, almost half a month's salary, and I could sense his distress. But he did not refuse me and had his secretary prepare an advance on his following month's salary so he could give me the money.

On the way from the church to the restaurant, the bus passed the gambling room on 63rd Street. Driven by an impulse, I got off at the next corner. I had about ten dollars of my own and if I could win $150 betting that amount, I might return the money at once to my father. Before entering the bookie's I sealed the envelope that contained my father's money and put it safely away in my pocket.

The first race I bet on seemed to confirm my anticipation of good fortune. I won $27. Another race was going off in a few moments with a sharp horse I had been following. Overlooked in the mutual betting, he was a tantalizing 10 to 1. I bet $30 on his nose to win. When he lost in a heart-wounding photo finish, raging at the taunting closeness of victory, I bet the remainder of my own money on a horse that ran third.

Unwilling to believe that I could have come so close if there were not favorable portents swirling about my head, I went into the small, reeking washroom and took out my father's envelope. I opened it carefully and took out a ten-dollar bill, making a futile effort to seal the envelope again. My parched mouth could not infuse the saliva to moisten the flap. I hurried to make my bet as the race was going off.

When I lost that race, fearful of having to explain the discrepancy between the $150 my father had given me and the $140 remaining, I made another trip to the washroom and emerged to make another bet. When I lost once more, I abandoned all reason and restraint in a frenzied scramble to regain the money he had given me.

I remember that afternoon as one of the most deranged and fevered days of my life. My father's money, half his salary for the following month, slipped away until with less than five dollars remaining of his $150, I stumbled out into the cold twilight. It had begun to snow, a light film of white flakes settling across the city. I stood in the alley, under the elevated tracks, and cried then for the waste and debris of my life.

When I finally returned to the lunchroom, I found the door locked and my wife waiting in the shadowed interior. I knocked on the glass and she opened the door, her cheeks frightened and pale.

In the darkened lunchroom, sitting beside one another on the stools, I told her what I had done. That too was an anguish I will never forget, that confession of shameful infirmity to my wife carrying our first child.

Somehow we managed to keep from telling my

father. We borrowed some money from my wife's sister and sold several of the appliances we had received as wedding presents.

In the days that followed I thought often of the old gambler, Gero Kambana, almost blind and nearly deaf, haunting the rooms where gamblers played. I saw the long terrible span of his life. In the brazier of his heart all other loves had grown pale and vanished under the brightness of a single consuming flame. In the end, hollowed and burned out, he was left without warmth, without love or hope, only loneliness and the savage riddle of thirty thousand days and nights.

Months would pass before I was free of my longings, months of small failures and tremulous fears. But in looking back I see that time as a kind of beginning, a renewal of my spirit when I understood I had to break free, because the alternative was for me to remain in a dark and corrosive bondage for as long as I lived.

X

THE SMALL, shabby lunchroom that I owned with a partner for a while and finally retained by myself had once been a barn in the younger days of the city. At certain dismal moments one could still smell the residue of horses that had somehow endured through a thousand scourings. In this porcine kingdom of four tables and twenty-three stools, a grease-blackened, coal-burning stove, and an octogenarian icebox built before the Civil War, I began a year of astringent unveilings.

My trade came mostly from the factories and railroads. There were also hoboes and drifters off the freights. Entering Chicago or stopping a while before moving on, they found my lunchroom a convenient spot for a cup of coffee and a bowl of soup. (This combination seemed to be the most filling and least expensive.)

They would wash the dust of a dozen states from their hands and faces in my battered kitchen sinks. Some were rascals and some were thieves and some

126

were men driven restlessly by their secret furies. It was hard to tell them apart, and in the beginning, they skewered me on the prongs of my own gullibility. I rapidly lost my innocence and became hardened to the endless tales of hardship, the interminable laments. I became less inclined to believe their stories, which were often graced with a bright versatility. Perhaps, like the wanderers of medieval times, they created a balladry of their own.

The man called Ed (I cannot recall the name he gave me then) came in on a Saturday afternoon. He was about fifty, of medium height, dressed in the drifter's shabby pants and worn jacket, neater than many others but unmistakably marked as a man down on his luck. He had thinning hair, a pale, tight-fleshed face, and eyes that glinted with the harried appeal of the wino. He managed the price of a bowl of soup, and I threw in a cup of coffee. It was a quiet part of the day, and in conversation he told me he was a chef, had been working at a hotel in Denver, had come to Chicago for a job.

I had a part-time cook, a taciturn Swede who prepared the few dinners I sold. I told Ed I could not use him. He lingered over his coffee, his manner growing more distraught, until during another lull he motioned me urgently back to his stool. He produced a baggage check from the freight department of the depot nearby, covering a suitcase he had sent

127

on ahead a week before. In the suitcase were clothing, some books, and his chef's knives. There was a dollar and a half due in storage charges, and Ed asked me to lend him the money and he would bring me the knives as security for repayment.

I wavered for a moment and then refused. My own situation was tenuous, the lunchroom business declining every day. I had heard some artful stories before and a number of times had been drawn into their nefarious web. A man gets tired of playing the fool.

I did not see him again for several days until an evening when he returned looking more harried and desperate than before. My dishwasher had left early that day, and there were some soiled dishes remaining in the sinks. Ed agreed to wash them. For a couple of hours he worked vigorously in the suds, afterwards swept the floor, growing more nervous as he sobered. I gave him the dollar and a half we had agreed upon for the two hours' work. I asked if he had redeemed his suitcase. When he told me he hadn't, I gave him another dollar and a half. He thanked me and left.

Several days later, early in the morning, when I opened the lunchroom, I found an envelope inserted under the door. The envelope contained Ed's baggage check, still unredeemed, an offering to compensate in some way for his violation of my trust.

I kept the baggage check in a compartment of my register for another two weeks, expecting him to return. When he did not appear, irritated at aiding his duplicity, I sent the dishwasher to the depot to retrieve the suitcase so it wouldn't be lost for storage charges. He returned with a shabby canvas bag, the lock broken and the clasps held together by a metal-buckled belt.

For almost three months the bag remained in a storage alcove off the kitchen. Finally, one evening after closing when I was alone, I decided Ed wasn't ever coming back. I opened the suitcase.

There were pieces of drab clothing, a pair of pants, a jacket, and a sweater—a lot that would bring fifty cents from one of the used-clothing stores along the nearby Skid Row. There were half a dozen books, including copies of Emerson's essays and Longfellow's poems, a few dog-eared menus from restaurants where he had apparently worked, and a half-dozen butcher knives of fair quality. There was also a slim packet containing some letters addressed to him at a restaurant in Denver. Because I had a sudden, strange foreboding, I thought of burning the letters unread. But I opened them because curiosity overcame my apprehension.

The first letter, dated about six months before, contained a black-and-white snapshot of an attractive light-haired woman and a girl of about ten. They stood frozen in the solemn rigidity of snapshots. The woman was Ed's wife and the girl his daughter and the letters were from them.

I read them and then, swept by sadness, read them again, fitting them together like fragments of a puzzle. Ed was an alcoholic, and all his anguished efforts to overcome his illness had failed. In a desperate effort to battle it out alone he had left his home in Los Angeles, taken the job in Denver, keeping his home and family a treasure that he had to earn by curing himself.

Yet, each of his wife's letters grew more frantic, scrawled appeals and pleas, reminding him of their love, asking him to return; they wanted him home under whatever shadow there might be rather than go on living without him.

The last letter of the four was dated about a week before he turned up in Chicago. His route suggested he was not going home but running farther away.

For weeks after that night I considered things I might do to help them. I talked to a policeman who ate on occasion in my lunchroom, and he took Ed's name and description and passed it around to some of the men who patrolled the bars and flophouses of Skid Row. But I never heard anything from their search. Several times I walked the streets of Skid Row myself, staring into the faces I passed, the men huddled in doorways for warmth. After a while I wasn't even sure I could have recognized him any more.

I tried to reassure myself that he might have made it somehow, that the love of his family had drawn him back from the brink of his hell, but I did not really believe that was true. I thought, finally, of writing his wife and then had to accept the burdened truth that I could write her nothing to console her. Perhaps she'd even condemn me for not having made a greater effort to save him.

I can never be certain, but perhaps the final glimpse I was given of Ed might well have been the last time he was recognized on this earth.

It took about a year of the long weary lunchroom hours and the floundering for a slim margin of profit among the scraps of food to batter me into wretched defeat. Desperate to get out from under the load and assisted by the ministrations of a disreputable real estate broker named Pericles (how the mighty have fallen), I sold the lunchroom to a pair of old Greeks out of Halsted Street.

Zakinthakis was a chef, a creator of dishes in the tradition of elegant cuisine. His treasures included a set of venerable knives and menus from a dozen major hotels and restaurants he had graced with his skill. Having grown old and slightly deaf, he could no longer work in their gleaming kitchens, but he had lost none of his pride.

His partner, Pappas, was a small bald man with skin the shade and texture of hardened grease. Although he had never been more than a counterman in lunchrooms as shabby as my own, his wife's death had left him a modest sum of insurance.

Pericles, the broker, convinced the two men who were strangers to one another that an alliance of talent and money would be fruitful. He accomplished the miracle of my liberation by driving a hard bargain. There was a small down payment and the remainder of the purchase price (much less than my partner and I had paid for the place) over a period of three years. I also had to agree to work with the partners for the first couple of weeks. Pericles fled counting his commission.

From the beginning, the partners were ardent in their hatred for one another. Zakinthakis, contemptuous of the untalented lout fate had pushed upon him, took undisputed charge of the kitchen. He scrubbed and polished the old blackened stove until a surface emerged that had not been visible in years. He installed new rubber lining on the icebox doors. He discarded my mundane and uninspired menu and began creating delicious specialties of his own. The freight handlers and factory workers continued to order hamburgers and cheeseburgers and despite the availability of some lovely raisin and sherry puddings, continued to request with implacable curiosity "W'at kind of pie ya got?"

Pappas shrieked in fury as he paid the bills. Since Zakinthakis had threatened to sever both his ears if he stepped foot into the kitchen, he cried out his threats and imprecations safely outside the kitchen door.

I tried to talk to the chef several times and make him understand that perhaps the neighborhood was not yet ready for his cuisine. He listened politely but remained adamant. He would open new vistas of culinary pleasure for our customers. He admonished me against losing faith.

That was in the middle of December, and when word was passed to us that the factories would work full shifts on Christmas Day, Zakinthakis conceived a bold plan to prepare a Christmas dinner worthy of Maxim's or the Waldorf and offer it to our customers at the price they would pay for an ordinary dinner. In this way they would become ardent converts to the efficacy of our menu. Zakinthakis, out of his own pocket, paid for the printing of a thousand handbills announcing the sumptuous treat, and, ignoring the vehement outrage of Pappas, he set about preparing for the great day.

It was an astonishing experience to see the chef at work. He moved as if he were a Renoir or Dégas among the cabbages and tomatoes, oranges and pears. Drab clusters of vegetables and fruit gained luster and beauty as they emerged from his hands. Driven by his faith into expecting a miracle, I washed the counters and tables and even polished some of the tarnished and battered silver.

In the last furious hours of preparation on Christmas Eve, an enigmatic and baleful quiet had descended upon Pappas. He seemed to sense that Zakinthakis had challenged destiny and he was content to watch and wait.

Christmas Day began slowly with a trickle of business involving no more than coffee and rolls. Several times, as the morning wore on, I noticed Zakinthakis in his clean white chef's hat peering through the partition from the kitchen. A few groups of customers entered for lunch, perhaps a dozen altogether, but as hard as I tried, I could not prevail upon more than one to order the special. That man ate the five courses quickly while reading his newspaper and paid without saying a word. We spent the remainder of the afternoon in a dreadful solitude. I sat at one of the tables while Pappas leaned on the cash register, his lips curled in a glittering smile. There wasn't a sound from the kitchen.

A little past eight o'clock, when we finally closed, I entered the kitchen for the first time since early afternoon. Zakinthakis was sitting in the corner beside the stove he had scrubbed and polished, his white hat folded in his lap. All about him were the untouched splendors of his dishes: the kettle of lemon soup, the trays of creamed and garnished potatoes, and the great garlanded ribs of meat. The look on his face was one of the most indescribable despair I had ever seen. Mute before his anguish, I took my coat and fled. Before I was even out the front door, Pappas had boldly entered the kitchen. I did not stay to hear his scornful shrieks, but I knew somehow, for the first time, Zakinthakis would not answer.

A day or so later they abandoned the lunchroom and I returned to salvage what I could. I sold off the battered fixtures to a restaurant supply house, and locked the door on the old barn for good.

For many years after that, particularly during the holidays, I remembered Zakinthakis. I reproached myself for a long time because I had not offered him a word of reassurance or comfort. But young as I was then, and not nearly wise enough in the ways of the artist and the world, what could I have said to console him?

XI

FROM Michigan Avenue and 61st Street, where my father's parish church was located, to the Woodlawn Hospital on Drexel Avenue is a span of about thirteen city blocks. My father passed the hospital on his way to church almost every day for twenty-six years. He died in the hospital after three months of confinement, on Memorial Day, 1951. I was in my twenties at the time, had been married five years with one son, my wife shortly to become pregnant with our second child.

For some years prior to my father's death, there had been dissension and bickering in the parish. Part of the turmoil was simply parish politics, one crafty faction seeking to impose their will upon another group equally as cunning. But there was also concern about the changing racial patterns of the neighborhood. Over the years, as the Negroes slowly broke free from the rigid environs that imprisoned them in ghettos, the church became an island in a Negro neighborhood. Many parishioners, including prominent members of the Board of Trustees, felt the parish buildings should be sold and a new church and school built elsewhere.

In the beginning my father opposed any sale and move. He knew the painful efforts required in building a new church. He had been through that experience years before when the original church had burned down. While conducting services in a nearby small Episcopalian church, my father and a group of parishioners pursued elusive mortgages and loans to finance the building of a new church. Many years were to pass before the last of the oppressive encumbrances had been paid off.

In addition, my father did not share the apprehension of some parishioners at the complexion of the neighborhood surrounding the church. When the first Negro families crossed South Park, for years a dividing line between white and black residences and apartments, a group of agitated white landlords brought my father a petition to sign, asking property owners to resist the invasion by refusing to rent or to sell to Negroes. They explained that although my father was not a property owner himself, his position as priest of the large Greek parish would add luster and force to the catalogue of signatures. My father listened courteously and then told them if they obtained his boss's signature, he would be permitted to sign.

137

"Your Bishop?" they asked.

"The Big Boss," my father said. "Jesus Christ."

Despite my father's objections, the church was sold. Plans were drawn envisaging the construction of a million-dollar church-school complex, a proposal my father felt was extravagant and unrealistic. For more than a year the parish was without a church, the various liturgies and services being held in borrowed churches, until a foundation and basement were constructed on the new site. When the basement had been roofed, an altar and iconostasion were set up at one end, and services were held there. After the projected construction ran into financing and contract difficulties, for a while it appeared they might never rise above the basement.

There were members of the Board of Trustees who complained that my father was not fund-raising for the new church with sufficient energy and dedication. My father responded that the years of labor had taken their toll, he suffered from diabetes and hypertension. The arguments, constant importunings for money from parishioners and banks, as well as the fetid and damp basement, did not improve his health. Finally, he took a month's leave of absence that year and a few weeks off in the one following. When he was reproved by the Board for these absences, he reminded them in a letter that for the first twenty-three years spent as a priest of the parish, he had never taken a vacation. Now, his health and general physical weariness required he do so. Disregarding their continued grumblings, at the end of the year, with services still being held in the chilled and comfortless basement, my father requested permission from the Archbishop and the Board of Trustees of the church for a year's leave of absence so he could "regain my health." He felt that the parish duties could be, for the most part, performed in his absence by the assistant Rector. He also admitted his fervent hope that by the time of his return, they would have emerged from the "catacombs, where Christianity began more than 2000 years ago."

The Board of Trustees called a general meeting to consider my father's request. After voting, the membership approved my father's request for a leave. They also authorized a payment to him for the year of $200 a month. This amount rankled those who would have preferred not to pay him anything, despite the common knowledge that my father had no savings and no other source of income except his salary to provide for my mother and himself. My father was also warned by friends that a small but powerful faction hoped the leave of absence might become a wedge to prevent him from returning to his parish. He could not believe that so harsh and ungrateful a tactic could be successful. He felt that

139

twenty-six years of devoted service to his church would weigh overwhelmingly in his favor.

A little over a year earlier, Naka dead, my older brothers and sisters living away from home, my father suggested that my wife, my son, and I move in with him. We would save the expense of separate rents, and if he were able to go away to rest, he would not leave my mother and younger sister alone. From this agreement came our purchase of a small, old house about a mile from the church for $16,500.

Since I had nothing to contribute to the down payment but enthusiasm, my father cashed in the $4000 he had managed to save in U.S. Savings Bonds during the war. This amount, added to his slim equity in the cottage, comprised his total savings and estate.

In December of 1949, when he had been granted his leave of absence, and after we had been living together for less than a year, he wrote a letter of farewell to the members of the parish asking them "to pray for our parish and for me in your prayers," promising that he would return to them at the end of the year, strengthened and refreshed. He left for California shortly after Christmas and soon afterwards began writing us warm and glowing letters from the desert community where he stayed.

STELMARK: *A Family Recollection*

"In all my life I have never experienced a lovelier and healthier climate. The sun burns as if it were the middle of July instead of March. The sky is as blue as the sky over Greece I have not seen for so many years but can still remember. We are 3000 feet above sea level and surrounded by mountains. There are no flies, no dust, no clouds or storms. Only a clean breeze that blows into the spirit and purifies me. O I cannot tell you how lovely it is here and how much better it makes me feel."

When he left the desert for the ocean community of Huntington Beach, he sent back snapshots showing himself clad in a mackintosh jacket and a floppy-brimmed hat, proudly holding aloft a string of slim, meager-fleshed fish. They were slightly larger fish than he used to catch in the lake near the cottage. He had purchased a rod and reel since those days, but he never really mastered or enjoyed the intricacies of casting. He remained a quiescent fisherman all his life, a bamboo pole and worm-on-the-hook man who realized as much pleasure from sitting in a boat and contemplating the cork bobbing gently in the water as he did in pulling up his catch.

But his idyllic sojourn in those early months of rest were shadowed by letters from friends who told him of plans to prevent his returning as Rector of the parish. There were rumors that another priest was being brought from Greece to replace him.

My father wrote letters to his supporters pledging

141

that with his health regained he would return and lead the fight against those who sought to oust him, to divide the community and besmirch the parish. In his letters to our family, he continued to write warmly of his surroundings, and yet he could not conceal his apprehension and his outrage.

"I thank God that he has brought me here to cleanse me of the poisons I have had to absorb from these men," he wrote us in April. "I feel myself growing stronger every day. When I am well again I promise you that I will return and kick some of the empty cans that clutter up the church."

His determination to retain his parish and his position as Rector was not simply a matter of pride. If he were forced to retire, there was no social security for priests at that time and no provision for any kind of pension.

As the weeks passed and it became irrevocably true that a priest was being brought from Greece to replace him as Rector, retiring my father on the fortune he had acquired during the years he had served the parish, he wrote us indignantly:

"Write me!" he demanded of my mother. "Write me the names of those people who claim I am wealthy, that I own acres of land, farms and apartment buildings. Write me so I can write them and ask the exact location of all this wealth I am supposed to have!"

As his bitterness mounted, he pungently assailed the men he felt were betraying him.

"I know the leader well. He composes the letters that others sign. He is a man without love in him, without any emotional understanding of human beings. And the duck, the monkey, the parrot, the weasel, and the nanny-goat do his bidding. God will punish them!"

A few paragraphs beyond he would ask:

"Why are they doing this terrible thing? What have I done to them that now that I am sick, they want to throw me out? Why, why, I ask myself over and over, why, why, and I cannot find any answer."

A week later he was in the hospital with a cold grown harsh and menacing in his chest. He wrote to reassure us that the confinement was precautionary and not serious. In a line near the end of that letter, he wrote:

"Sometimes I feel so heavy a resignation I don't know what to do."

In October of that year he returned from California to Chicago to plan and, as he said, "take charge of my program to return to my church." He knew the priest from Greece had arrived and had

143

been installed in the parish, and was conducting services. But there had been no formal notification to my father about the replacement. My father could not believe that when the year's leave of absence was over, he would not be allowed to return to his church. Meanwhile he waited, wrote endless letters, attended conferences with friends, sought support, argued and pleaded. He alternated between spells of brooding and of confidence, between fits of indignation and of helplessness.

On those nights when restlessness would prevent his sleeping, I'd come off the midnight-to-dawn shift at the steelmill where I had been working for some months and find him at the dining-room table in our house. There was his small black attaché case on the chair beside him, and numerous letters and carbons of letters spread out before him. He assembled all the memos and correspondence concerning his leave of absence and his return to his church in the attaché case. He carried the case up and down the stairs endlessly, from his bedroom to the dining room, even keeping it beside him at the small telephone stand when he made a call.

There was an evening when several family friends, one of them a young attorney, came to our house to discuss the situation with my father. My father once again recited his position and his complaint, his voice trembling as he read passages from the various letters, the evasive sentences from members of the Board of Trustees, the noncommittal syntax from the Archbishop in New York.

At the end, the attorney, who was genuinely fond of my father, and who had become agitated through the recital, burst out.

"You want to know what legal position you got, Father?" the attorney cried. "You got shit! That's what you got, Father, shit! No contract, no guarantee they'll allow you to go back to your church, no pension or money of any kind if they don't want to give it to you! All you got is shit!"

My father understood English well enough to comprehend the miasmic composition of shit, and he nodded mutely and sadly. And the attorney, remorseful after his outburst, advised my father to write a letter to the Board of Trustees, informing them officially that he had returned from his leave of absence and was fully prepared to assume his duties as spiritual leader of his parish on January 1 of the New Year.

On the 18th of December my father notified the Board of Trustees of his desire to resume his duties at the beginning of the New Year as Rector of the Church that, he reminded them, he had served faithfully for twenty-six years.

Through the holidays that year, my father somehow managed to retain faith that things would work

145

out all right, that duplicity and cunning would be vanquished. The Archbishop in New York would intervene on his behalf. The Bishop in Chicago would help him. Above all else, he relied upon the spiritual covenants he had formed with the members of his congregation. For more than a quarter of a century he had listened to their confessions, married their sons and daughters, baptized their grandchildren, spoken final words over their dead. He had shared the dark burden of their despair. If he were older, not as well as he had been, he needed their solace and support as they had so often needed his prayers and service. He knew they would not willingly forsake him, even as he ruefully understood that a group of wealthy and determined men were directing and leading the affairs of the parish.

"I am not asking for charity," he said over and over. "I want my justice. If I do not have the strength or the health I had once, neither am I worthless. I served my church for twenty-six years and they have no right to throw me out, unconcerned with how I live and care for my family. I want my justice."

In early January, the Board of Trustees met to consider the matter of my father's return. Two days later the mail brought the certified letter with their decision.

146

"The Board of Trustees carefully considered your request for reappointment as Rector of the Church, and carefully weighed the fine and loyal service which you rendered to the congregation over the past years, also your present state of health and your present ability to adequately serve the community. It was the resolution of the Board of Trustees that it would not be to the best interest of your health or to the best interest of the community to reappoint you as Rector of St. Constantine Church. The feeling of the members of the Board was that the requirements, duties and responsibilities of the position would impose too great a demand upon your physical stamina. The Board further resolved that as of December 31, 1950, your duties and responsibilities as Rector and your leave of absence would be terminated."

In thee, O Lord, do I put my trust: let me never be put to confusion.

"The members of the Board further considered your own financial requirements and resolved that you were to be paid the sum of $200.00 per month from January 1, 1951, to December 31, 1951, and that before December 31, 1951, the Church would again consider the financial condition of the Church and your financial requirements and determine whether or not any further contribution would be paid to you. The Board of Trustees, as further recognition of your long, faithful and excellent service to the Congregation, resolved that you be designated as Rector Emeritus of the St. Constantine Hellenic Orthodox Church, and that your name appear as Rector Emeritus on all the stationery of the Community."

147

Harry Mark Petrakis

Deliver me in thy righteousness, O Lord, and cause me to escape: incline thine ear unto me and save me . . . for mine enemies speak against me; and they that lay wait for my soul take counsel together.

"The Board of Trustees further resolved that the foregoing provisions, pension payment and title were granted on the condition that you find them agreeable and acceptable, and were willing to abide by them, and that you would cooperate with the Board of Trustees and the Rector to the best interest of the Church and the Community."

Deliver me, O my God, out of the hand of the wicked, out of the hand of the unrighteous and cruel man.

"In order to conclude the matter and commence the payment of your pension at the earliest possible date, we would appreciate your acknowledging receipt of the original of this letter and indicating your acceptance hereof in the space provided therefor on the copy of the letter which is enclosed herewith, and returning the copy to the office of the Church in the enclosed envelope."

Cast me not off in the time of old age; forsake me not when my strength faileth.

"On behalf of the members of the Congregation and the Board of Trustees, I extend to you our deepest and sincerest appreciation and gratitude for the fine and excellent service which you have rendered to our Community in the past, and we hope and pray you will soon be restored to full health."

148

STELMARK: *A Family Recollection*

O God, be not far from me: O my God, make haste for my help . . . Save me, O God, for the waters are come in unto my soul . . .

How many times my father read that letter, slowly and with effort, or had us read it to him, I do not know in numbers. But those first days after it arrived, we came to memorize each word and line as if they were a catechism. "What does that word mean?" he'd ask. "What does the line explain?" "Read that sentence to me again."

As we read and explained the sentences again, his pride and dignity suffered fresh wounds. He'd go alone to another room, to sit in the darkness for a while. We walked softly and gravely about the house, feeling the waves of his despair.

I was grateful to go to work, to leave the house for a few hours. When I returned home we'd be back at the letter once more. He'd ask me to read it to him again, trying in futile, whirling repetition to understand why he was being driven from the house of his Lord.

"What does that word mean?" "What does the line explain?" "Read that sentence to me again."

Through the remainder of January and into the early part of February, my father would not sign and return the letter. As a result he received no salary

149

from the first of the year. He worried about the expenses of the house that he knew could not be sustained on my wages alone, or even on my wages and the tenuously renewable pension they offered him. He continued to solicit support, addressing urgent letters to the Archbishop in New York asking "for my justice."

In a final, canonized encyclical, the Archbishop wrote my father that settlement of the matter hinged on the question of whether or not my father was able to function, fully and completely, as Rector, performing all, not simply part, of his duties with unflagging energy and constant activity. He could not waver or lapse in servicing the economic, educational, spiritual, intellectual, and moral needs of the community. He must visit the sick in the hospitals, visit the homes and stores of the Christians for the purpose of preaching and teaching the faith and to offer his congratulations on their holy name days. If my father deemed himself able to meet this demanding schedule, the Archbishop first required the sworn affidavits of two competent doctors (to be selected by the Board of Trustees) who would examine my father and attest to his unqualified fitness to resume his duties (that would exhaust the strength of even a young, strong priest). The letter ended with the Archbishop's paternal and affectionate blessings.

A little more spirit was driven from my father's

body, and he went through his days and nights in a kind of numbed and querulous wonder. Still he could not bring himself to sign and return the letter.

There was an afternoon in the middle of February when I sat watching television, my son playing at my feet, and my father came home. He had gotten a haircut and he took off his black hat and his shorn scalp made his head look stripped and misshapen. He sat down for a moment to play with my son, and I brought him his slippers and untied and removed his shoes.

"Is there any wrestling on the television now?" he asked.

I told him no, and he rose and walked upstairs slowly, to go to bed, he said, because he was not feeling well. He remained in bed for several days and then, feeling better, came downstairs for a few hours at a time in his robe and slippers. He'd sit quietly staring out the windows at the cold, bleak February day.

During this period of my father's confinement, the Archbishop from New York arrived to visit him. His Eminence had been informed his brother in Christ was ailing, and he swept into our house, robed and bearded, a benign and solicitous apostle of mercy. For almost four hours he and my father were locked behind the closed parlor doors. Afterwards the Arch-

151

bishop emerged, invoking his blessings upon our house and upon us before he departed.

A few days later the last of the letters written by the Board of Trustees to my father arrived in the mail. The Archbishop had hastened to them with the joyous tidings. Expressing the Board's gratitude and sincere appreciation for my father's pledge of cooperation to the Archbishop, they were delighted to agree to certain modifications in their original letter. In return for my father's acceptance of the new priest as undisputed Rector of the parish, they would allow my father to officiate at Mass once a month, if he were able and so desired, also to perform baptisms, weddings, and funerals when the involved parties requested him. He would be, as they had promised, designated Rector Emeritus, his name appearing as such on the church stationery, and as evidence of their good faith, they enclosed the check of the church in the amount of $200.

My father went back to bed for almost a week. The doctors worried about pneumonia and made plans to move him to the Woodlawn Hospital. The last afternoon he was home, as we waited for the ambulance, a group of old women from his parish came to visit him. They sat in a row of chairs at the foot of his bed, the only light in the room a faint glow from a small lamp. When I entered the bedroom to bring my father one of his medicines and a glass of water and bent over him, I saw him watching the silent, dark-garbed women with a curious intensity. I realized then how much they resembled dark crows or ravens, drawn together in some ancient, premonitory ritual of a death-watch about his bed.

My father lived in the hospital for three months. They were months in which he endured unremitting pain, needles taped into his veins and iridescent bottles and coils strung like plumes about his bed. The flesh melted from his body until all that remained was transparent skin stretched tightly over a network of his bones. Yet, his anger and bitterness burned away, as well, until by the end he radiated an awesome tranquillity and calm acceptance at the imminence of death.

My mother absorbed the brunt of my father's confinement, spending the entire day, every day, with him. My sisters and I visited him at odd times during the day to sit with him for a while.

He had always enjoyed reclining in bed and talking. During the years we lived together, on those nights he was in bed and he'd hear me coming in the front door, he'd call me into his room. My mother might be up late baking in the kitchen and I'd slump wearily on the edge of her bed. Across from me in the other twin bed my father would read me a passage from a newspaper or book. Since he always regretted not having mastered English, there were English vocabulary and grammar books on the table beside his bed. Sometimes he'd ask me to listen as he read one of the lessons so I might correct his errors. We made plans to work regularly at these lessons. He remained eager and willing, but I think he understood that I felt it was a chore, so we stopped after a session or two. But one of the books he carried to the hospital was an English vocabulary text. As if to make up for all the times I had avoided the lessons, I asked him to read from the text so I might correct him. He would try for a few moments, until weariness made him stop.

He talked, often, of California, his voice shaken with nostalgia for the sun and the desert, the clear, serene passage of days. I promised him that after he was well, we'd take my mother, my wife and son, and move the family to California. The prospect of that seemed to please him.

There were many times, especially as the weeks went on, when drugs and pain rendered him inert and silent, I'd sit beside his bed, trying to find something to say to reassure him and myself, yearning to leave so I would not have to see his veins, swollen and purple along his wrists, the pulse that wriggled like a small dark worm in his forehead. Worst of all was the smell of decay like a rank mist from his body. I couldn't understand how my mother endured the endless hours she spent with him. After sitting with him a while, I'd lie to him about an appointment or an errand that prevented my staying longer. He never complained about my departures, never tried to detain me, but urged me to go and meet my obligations.

Sometimes I grew angry at the measure of his suffering, resenting his acceptance of the cathartic qualities of pain. When I lamented what he was being forced to endure, he reproached me softly.

"I have done things, harbored thoughts, spoken words for which I am ashamed," he told me. "Now God gives me a chance to clean myself of these poisons."

In accordance with that conviction he sent for men from the parish, men he had denounced as his enemies. He forgave them and asked each one of them to forgive him.

Still, incredibly, he clung to life. His body became a pale and pearly filament of flesh that the thrust of a finger might rupture. Through it all his eyes remained warm and alive, glowing with what he must have known were his final days of life. There were nights when the doctors called the family to the hospital, telling us gravely they did not expect him to survive the night. All of us believed them, except my mother, who knew my father best of all. We'd gather silently in the shadowed corridor outside his

155

room, seeking to console one another through the long hours of the night. In the morning my father was, somehow, miraculously alive.

On those days he felt a little stronger, he enjoyed sitting by the window in his room, looking across the roofs of the buildings toward the faintly visible spire and belltower of the old church that had been sold. Since he no longer had the strength to walk, on these occasions I lifted him from the bed and carried him to the armchair by the window. His wasted body seemed to float in my arms.

On such a day, alone with him in the room, as I carried him the few feet from his bed to the arm- chair, he rested his cheek against my cheek. "As I once carried you in my arms," he said softly, "now you carry me."

He died a few days later, quietly in his sleep, a short while after my mother had left the hospital to come home.

For three days my father's body, attired in the gilded, colorful robes of his vestments, lay in state in a casket sealed under glass. For three days several thousand people passed through the catacombs, the damp basement of the church, circling his casket, crossing themselves, kissing the glass above his heart. Many of them were the parishioners whose confes- sions he had heard for more than a quarter of a

156

century, whose sons and daughters he had married, whose grandchildren he had baptized, and over whose dead he had spoken final words. He had often shared the dark burden of their despair, and they came now in solemn, grieving lines to offer him their solace and support.

And like an awed and silent menagerie, the man without love in him, the parrot, the duck, the monkey, the weasel, and the nanny-goat took turns standing about his bier. I was swept with bitterness and fury at the sight of them, and for a while I thought of crying out against them, driving them away. I remained silent during those long days because I realized that if my father had made his peace with life, I had no sanction to carry hatred over into his death. I kept silent, also, because I knew nothing they had done to him surpassed what I had done to him because he loved me and was vulnerable before that love in a way he could never have been with strangers.

But I am grateful for those months of my father's dying, for those hours with him that I twisted to avoid, for they bequeathed me a compact of recognition. Nothing I had experienced in my life to the time of my father's death had grieved me more, no loss more severe for me than the pain of losing him. Yet, long after his death, I can clearly remember his pale face, his slender-fingered hands, his warm eyes, and the gentle whisper of his voice as he spoke longingly of the sun in the desert.

I have come to understand that in those anguished moments when we are torn by love and loss, a part of us stands aside, absorbing words, sounds, movements, the firmament of joy and grief, so it is never forgotten. And for a writer, this divisible yet indivisible bond between memory and the writing of stories makes a requiem of death and provides those who have died with a legacy that lives on.

To the very end and beyond, the old man paid me far more than he ever received from me, leaving the ledger of our lives together imbalanced in my favor.

And with each of my stories and books, I try again to make an entry and an adjustment on his page.

XII

I BEGAN WRITING casually, almost indifferently, when I was still a child, impressed by the rhythms of words and by their effect on adults. During Thanksgiving and Christmas and Easter holidays, I scribbled quick, effortless poems that my father delighted in having me read before the captive guests assembled at our table. The verses were simple and artless, unsuspicious of any discordance beneath the surface of life. The first two lines (all I can remember, fortunately) of one such poem began:

> Here we sit drinking wine at the table
> From a bottle with a bright red label . . .

Barely literate, but from the applause my passionate recitation drew from my father and the guests, one would suppose my creation ranked beside the hallowed poetry of Longfellow and Tennyson.

The two years of my illness gave me the chance to read voraciously, garlanding my vocabulary with

159

numerous words I could not pronounce, enabling me to accumulate a swarm of facts, events, and theories, all unmoored in the puddles of my imagination but there, someday, to be trickled into the stream.

I took for granted that I was going to be a writer. After my illness, confirming my expectation, I was designated storyteller laureate of my seventh-grade class at our parochial school. I was often called upon to read my stories before the class, and my teacher, with uncommon consideration for the literary sensibilities of my classmates, retained my readings for last.

When my turn came to walk to the podium at the front of the room, an unmistakable flutter of anticipation swept from the desks of the eager students. I would wait until the room was absolutely silent, meanwhile savoring the warm, admiring smile of a dark-eyed lovely plum of a girl sitting at a desk in the first row.

I'd begin to read my story, pitching my sentences slowly and carefully into the attentive stillness that gripped the room. At the end of the reading I'd steal a quick, longing glance at the plum of a girl in the first row, feeling my heart washed in the radiance of her cheeks. I'd walk back to my seat through waves of applause, affecting a demeanor of modesty even as one of my eyes, slitted and baleful, glared

160

at some lout more restrained in his clapping than the rest.

These balmy and delirious triumphs were midnight snacks I retasted in the last few moments before falling asleep, my ears ringing again with the echoes of that heady approval. What joy, I thought, what jolly happiness was a writer's life!

Despite the fact that I had read enough of the old Greek tragedies, I could not divine that the relentless gods might punish hubris in Chicago as well as in Thebes. My retribution came about one day at the beginning of the noon hour when my teacher asked me why I had no lunch. I was suddenly appalled at the banal flatness of having to answer, "I forgot it at home." My imagination took flight like a gull. I began explaining that on my way to school that morning I noticed a forlorn old man sitting in the gutter. Moved by his obvious misery, I asked him was was wrong. When he told me he had not eaten in two days, I gave him my lunch.

My teacher was so impressed by my unselfish charity she sent for the principal and had me repeat the story for him and the class. With a storyteller's fertile conjurings I added a number of flourishes. I detailed the man's wretchedness, his ragged, torn clothing, the broken seams of his shoes. I described his fingers trembling with gratitude as he accepted

161

the bag of lunch, the tears in his eyes as he made an effort to thank me.

When I had finished the story, the class was so overwhelmed and awed that they neglected to applaud. The principal shook my hand firmly. The dark-eyed, lovely plum of a girl in the first row cried. I returned to a desk crammed with liverwurst, salami, and cheese sandwiches, chocolate chip cookies and Lorna Doones, gleaming apples, oranges, and one juice-glutted peach. I gazed upon the bountiful harvest and for a few moments believed the rewards were deserved, if not for the morality of my pretended action, at least for the versatility of my imagination.

I had no premonition of disaster when the classroom door opened a few moments later and my mother entered. I was not surprised to see her, because she came to church often for a meeting or to visit my father. My teacher rose and greeted her warmly. And my mother handed her the bag of lunch I had forgotten at home that morning.

I have blocked the horror of the next few moments so effectively from my memory, I cannot honestly recall what took place. Perhaps it is best that way. Even in Greek tragedy, Medea murders her children offstage. I do recall, however, that the sheer immensity of my deception gilded my chastised head for months. In the schoolyard, hallways, and class-

162

rooms, I was pointed out with awe as "the biggest liar in the world." And for a long time after that fateful day, if I entered my classroom dripping wet, holding a drenched umbrella, and remarked that it was pouring down rain, everybody turned to look out the windows and make sure.

As I graduated from elementary school and entered high school, I continued in a euphoric assurance that if I never raised another pencil, or struck another typewriter key, publication and literary success would come whining like puppies at my heels, begging for the savory biscuits of my prose.

At about the age of eighteen, when my obsession with gambling began, my writing and dreams of literary success were submerged in more immediate excitements. This exile lasted until the second year of my marriage, after the abortive venture into the lunchroom.

I am not sure why I started to write again. Perhaps it came about as a clumsy, desperate effort to relieve the terror I felt about my life that seemed out of control. I started putting stories down on paper almost as a kind of religious ritual to exorcize my devils. For whatever the reasons, taunted with vague longings and frail memories, I tried for several dismal months to refurbish the confidence I once felt about writing. But I had lost the ability to bridge the chasm between reality and make-believe. The years of gambling had rooted me to the earth; the indulgent, undisciplined years when I fashioned parlays in place of sentences had scooped me out, left me hollow and homesick.

I also came, grimly, to learn the difference in the reactions to a child's composing of stories and similar endeavors by an adult. In the steelmills, during the occasional night shift when the plate mill was down, I sat in a corner of the scheduling office and tried to scribble fragments of a story.

"What you doing?" a burly stoker asked me one night.

"Writing."

"Letter?" he asked.

"A story," I said, perhaps recalling the approbation the act had received from my classmates and family.

His big, open-palmed hand slapped my papers to the floor.

"What in hell are you?" he said harshly. "A goddam queer!"

I retrieved my papers silently, accepting his condemnation as containing a shame I could not perceive. After that night I learned to conceal my writing, and when questioned, to evade answering the truth.

I moved from the steelmills to work in the consumer complaint department of a firm that manufactured floor waxes and furniture polishes. In this environment I was encouraged to write.

Dear Madam:

We received your letter of March 16 and were sincerely dismayed to read of your unhappy experience with our furniture polish. We cannot understand why the stains should not have been removed, but we want to assure you that we stand behind our money-back guarantee, therefore . . .

Sometimes on those afternoons when I pushed my baby son in his buggy along the lake, I stared across the haze above the water and wondered fitfully what legacy I might someday have to leave him. The task of writing seemed overwhelming, every small beginning fraught with inexorable labor and despair, my hands and heart useless, bungling tools. Since I could never succeed at writing, despite some pain, I relinquished my fool's dream by simply ceasing to write.

In an effort to rediscover a new direction, I resumed my schooling. I enrolled in evening courses at various downtown schools, studying history, philosophy, and the guitar. Because I had a fairly resonant voice, I considered the field of radio and television and signed up for courses at a school for broadcasting. I had classes in news editing, sports announcing, and dramatic writing. In the seventh or eighth week of the fall semester, one of the assign-

165

ments in the writing class was a 1500-word story on a theme related in some way to Christmas.

For the first time in almost a year, I wrote a story again, composing it one evening at home and desultorily revising it the following night. I wrote of a waiter returning home from work on Christmas Eve, carrying a small pine tree and a few presents for his wife. Finding his apartment dark and deserted, he conducts a familiar search in the taverns along the street and finds his wife drunk with another man. He takes her back to their apartment and slaps her without any real fervor. Afterwards, remorseful, he carries her to bed, undresses and washes her, and sits beside her until she has fallen asleep. Then he decorates the tree he had brought home, spreads the presents he had bought for her beneath it, and goes to bed anticipating the few hours of warmth and pleasure they would share in the morning.

Several manuscripts, including mine, were selected at random to be read. When my turn came and I walked to the front of the classroom, I could not help remembering the buoyant journeys of my youth, my confidence and excitement. But the dark-eyed, lovely plum of a girl who once smiled at me from the front row was gone, in her place an austere-lipped, middle-aged man with tufts of hair sprouting like the stems of radishes from his ears. In that mournful moment,

a century away from the playgrounds of my childhood, I read my story.

There was a long, tight silence after I had finished.
I wondered, anxious and fearful, if the class so dis-
liked my story that they had been rendered mute.
As they slowly began describing their reactions, I
understood with bewilderment and a massive relief
that my teacher and the class had been intemperately
moved.

In the excited discussion that followed, many of
the students argued that the story must have been
true, written from the anguish of personal experience,
the only reason they could have been so affected.
When I insisted the story was fiction, they simply assumed I was trying to conceal my shame and protect
my afflicted wife.

After the class that night I walked the deserted
winter paths of the park across from the school, staring at the street lamps that glittered frostily in the
sluggish air. The night, the trees, and the cold
formed a curious harmony in my body, a reconciliation between who I was and what I wanted to be.
The years of digressions, impediments, and confusions were suddenly cleared away. I swore my soul
and my hands to writing once again.

I was about twenty-four years old when I resumed
the struggle to cast and fashion stories from words

that creaked and strained like hinges and bolts rusted on a door sealed for years. Through a number of fitful and abortive spasms I managed to finish a story that I typed carefully and sent away to a magazine whose address and editor's name I had obtained from a writer's magazine. When it came back three weeks later, there was a small printed rejection slip clipped to the title page. "We are sorry . . ."

I wrote a second story, and then a third. By that time the first story had been rejected several more times and I retyped the frayed pages and sent them out again. I discovered the cursed expense of postage when an amount equal to that on the outside of the envelope had to be affixed to the self-addressed envelope enclosed within. As fast as a story was returned, I'd get it back into the mail again, hoping by sheer quantity to improve my chances of acceptance. But all that happened was that six stories returned as quickly as one. Besides the inevitable rejection slips, there were other indignities. One magazine took the first-class postage off my return envelope and replaced it with third-class postage. I imagined the vultures growing wealthy making similar substitutions on the thousands of manuscrips they received each week. When the magazine folded a few years later, I felt their punishment was deserved.

Over the months the printed rejection slips stretched out like the pages of a calendar. After about a year of futile submissions I was forced to accept the grim truth that my stories, singly or together, could not assess the value of a dozen empty pop bottles that littered the garbage, since the bottles could, if redeemed, at least bring a few pennies.

During this time, in order to live and support my wife and son, I stumbled through a procession of dreary jobs. I labored on the baggage platforms of the Railway Express, unloading mail cars with mufflers wrapped double around my ears and nose, a visor of wool futile against the stinging wind and bitter cold. After I quit, in an effort to melt the glaciers that rooted in the marrow of my bones, I went to work in the small, nest-warm shop of a tailor with yellow eyes and lopsided ears who taught me the rudiments of pressing clothes. That lasted until I nearly expired inhaling the stink of steam floating up through dried excrement and urine on men's pants. (You got a heavy foot, the tailor told me when I resigned. Try castor oil and barley water.)

There was a brief stint in a drugstore, and then I answered an ad for training as a typewriter repairman. Feeling that occupation suggested affinity with my desire to write, I went to the factory where a clerk took me to see the plant foreman. We walked through a massive shop containing several hundred workbenches where men labored over the dismembered spleen and glands of typewriters while others tested assembled machines in an ear-piercing roar. The place seemed the heartland of bedlam, the occupants a horde of madmen. The foreman wasn't in his office, and the clerk went to find him. The moment he disappeared among the benches, I turned and fled back the route we had come.

That was one job I escaped, but there were others I caught and lasted at only a few months. Part of the problem was simply that I didn't want to work. The moment I landed a job I began scheming for ways to justify quitting so I could salvage a few weeks of writing full-time before going back to another job. The irony was that when I finally quit or was fired, the insecurity and pressing bills battered me into a morose immobility. I wrote no more during these periods than I had written while employed. And every time I returned to work I had to renew a sardonic ritual of confession. On the applications for new employees, under the listing *Previous Positions,* I had to fill in:

Hired April 1946—Left June 1946
Hired August 1946—Left December 1946
Hired February 1947—Left June 1947
Hired June 1947—Left September 1947
Hired December 1947—Left April 1948
Hired June 1948—Left October 1948

170

Since there were rarely spaces for more than three or four previous jobs, I kept running off the bottom of the application. One personnel manager, after examining my record, looked across the desk at me with a kind of awe. "Jesus Christ!" he said fervently. "What's wrong with you?"

He was prudent to ask, since it was a question I often asked myself. Looking around at friends and casual cronies, I could not discern any pattern of employment remotely resembling my own erratic flip from job to job. One of the fellows I knew had gone to prison for stealing several adding machines from the offices where he worked, but even he had been employed with the company for five years before committing the crime.

My family suffered through these reversals. My wife became adept at keeping the gas, electric, and telephone companies from discontinuing our services by telling them, "We have a sick child at home." She might have been referring to me.

And when my mother went to a tea or a luncheon and met the mothers of other boys I had gone to school with, she'd have to listen to them expound on the achievements of their offspring. Eventually the conversation came around to me.

"Where is Harry working now?"

My mother would struggle to classify my current position in the best possible light.

"He's employed for a big company on Cicero Avenue," my mother said.

"Someone was telling me he's working for a brewery."

My mother nodded in resignation.

"In the office?" the friend might press relentlessly.

My mother accepted the fact that her position in the community as the wife of the priest consigned her to the truth.

"On a truck," she said.

If there is scant social approval for the aspiring writer, a greater dilemma exists because it is almost impossible for the usual creative writing teachers to teach the new writer to write. They can tutor him in grammar and direct his reading to the books of good writers, but they cannot teach him to construct a valid character or create a cogent story. He has to find his way through that twisting labyrinth alone by long and hard work.

I learned these grim truths, with one exception, when I signed up for courses in writing. The teachers were well-intentioned, haphazardly qualified men and women who had never written themselves (although they had degrees in literature and English) or were the authors of inspirational articles, obscure essays, memorabilia, gossamer poetry, and the history of lakes and mountains, towns and rivers. One adulated

172

STELMARK: *A Family Recollection*

Virginia Woolf and scorned Ernest Hemingway. Another lavished inordinate praise on Henry James and sought to have us model our writing on his meticulous obfuscations. Still another teacher sought to funnel our diverse styles into a smooth, cloying farrago that would somehow adhere to the palates of the editors of *Woman's Home Companion*. I never completed any of the writing courses I began, and if there are benefits I somehow garnished from the time spent in those classes, they remain concealed from me to this day.

The exception I mentioned was a private teacher of writing whose office was in her home on the South Side of Chicago. Marjorie Peters, a writer and agent, was a slender, sensitive woman with a generous spirit who really cared for words and loved writing. For a number of months one winter I walked across the vacant lot that separated our apartments in Hyde Park to sit beside her on a couch spread with numerous pillows. An electric heater glowed at our feet to combat the chill of the rooms after the heat had been turned down. Weary from her own long day of teaching and writing, she donated several hours of her night, on many nights, gently endeavoring to impress upon me the need for discipline and self-criticism. Despite the relevant fact that I had no money to pay for these instructions, she helped me anyway.

The most difficult part of writing for me then, as it

173

remains the most arduous to this day, was revising, the careful reworking of a story after the emotional explosion that produces a first draft. Writing in the heat of feeling was hard enough, but to return to the pages after the heat had cooled and see the words one thought diamonds and pearls become gimcracks and baubles is a somber and demoralizing experience.

To drill myself in these painful overhaulings, I borrowed or devised a series of exercises. Using photographs of men and women, country and city scenes, I'd begin by describing each photo in a paragraph of prose. I'd keep paragraph and photo in a folder. From time to time I'd select one of the folders and rework that particular paragraph, expanding the visual description and introducing smells and sounds not visible in the photo but inherent in the scene. I'd also try to create an aura of the mood the scene suggested to me, whether of sadness or of joy. Then I'd grapple with the arduous problem of cutting, of reworking what I wanted to say in fewer, sharper words.

Yet, despite all my truncating and ripening skills, I could not sell a story. I continued to write them and mailed them off to the magazines. They kept coming back in the envelopes I enclosed with each submission. Most of the time the rejections were the impersonal, printed comments, but from time to time a reader or an editor penned a notation suggesting there was someone alive on the staff of the magazine. *Partisan Review* said, "Sorry." *The Antioch Review* said, "Well told." *Redbook* Magazine said, "Nicely done." *The Sewanee Review* said, "My sincere apologies for my very long delay in reporting; I've been recalled to duty in the Navy and am finding it difficult to keep up with my reading." *Harper's Magazine,* with a printed rejection slip that included the sentence, ". . . the volume of manuscripts received is so great that we are obliged, for lack of editorial space, to decline many which are ably written and publishable," once returned such a slip rejecting a story with the words "ably written and publishable" underlined. In the margin someone had written, "Sorry we haven't time to help you. Good luck elsewhere." I treasured that rejection slip and for weeks carried it folded in my wallet.

As months went by and my submissions continued, certain editors began responding to my work with personally written comments. These letters and notes did not merely warm me by substituting a human being in place of the asphyxiating anonymity of the printed rejections, but by their clear, pointed observations helped uncover weaknesses I could not discern in my own work. I will never forget some of these editors: George Wiswell of *Esquire,* Esther Shiverick and Edward Weeks of *The Atlantic,* Eleanor Rawson of *Collier's,* Ray Russell and Pat

Pappas of *Playboy,* Paul Bixler of *The Antioch Review.* On a few occasions one of these editors suggested I revise my story and try them again. I set furiously to work, altering and reshaping as if my life depended upon the outcome. The revisions must have shown my desperation, because all were turned down.

Besides my wife, no one suffered as much with my labors as my father. Unable to fully understand my stories, his love mustered complete faith in my eventual success. He kept some of my manuscripts in the desk of his office at church. When visitors entered his office, he'd take the stories from his drawer as if, published or unpublished, they proved the existence of a mighty talent. "My son has written these stories," he'd say with obvious pride. "He's going to be a great writer someday." Out of respect for my father, the visitors discreetly kept their considerable skepticism about my future to themselves.

When my father died, he left a meager sum of insurance, less than $3000, plus the $200 a month his church had voted to continue paying to my mother until the end of the year. That sum and the insurance money dried up at about the same time, and the responsibility of house and family landed on my improvident head. Deprived of the bulwark of my father's presence, his soft, wry humor, his love and faith in me, I was a brawny and man-sized child

176

suddenly thrust into the world alone. For the next five years I sought to replace my father as the mainstay of a house we were perpetually on the brink of losing, while continuing to write stories I could not sell.

If numerous frustrations stuck like the quills of porcupines in my craggy flesh during these years, few afforded me the sheer matchless misery I derived from our family business, begun by my mother after my father's death. Although the return was nominal, an average of about $150 a month, this amount paid the light and gas bills on the house and allowed my mother to send a few dollars each month to poor relatives and friends in Greece.

The business, which began modestly and thrived, was the preparing of large trays of Koliva, the boiled, dried, and sugar-garnished wheat used in the Greek Orthodox Church as part of the memorial services for the dead. As the wheat, when planted, sprouts from the earth, the Koliva symbolized the souls of the dead that would rise from their graves for rebirth and salvation. Through her capable and energetic labors in obtaining orders and making the Koliva, my mother helped numerous old friends rest in peace. If Death never took a holiday, neither did my mother.

Like a secret rite of some aboriginal tribe, pre-

177

paring the Koliva required that the dried kernels of wheat be boiled in great kettles of water all day Saturday. The starch from the wheat formed a pungent, bubbling crust on the surface of the water which had to be skimmed off. The brew had to be stirred frequently with a long wooden spoon to keep the kernels from adhering to the bottom of the kettle. After the kernels had become tender, the kettle was lugged to the sink or a laundry tub, the viscid, sticky water drained off, the kernels rinsed a number of times, and then spread on large cloths to dry. That completed Saturday's labor.

Early Sunday morning my wife and mother began again. My mother browned sesame seed and flour in a shallow baking pan while my wife lined a large silver tray with wax and paper doilies. The sesame seed was mixed into the wheat, and then chopped walnuts, cinnamon, shredded parsley, and sweet white seedless currants were added. This mixture was then piled into a mound on the doilies of the tray. A half-dozen boxes of confectioner's powdered sugar were sprinkled over the mound and pressed down gently with wax paper to make a smooth and compact frosting of sugar. A cross and the initials of the deceased were outlined in the sugar and then slowly and painstakingly decorated with tiny silver dragées, each one placed gently to avoid marring the smoothness of the sugar surface. That completed the labor except for the delivery of the tray or trays to church early Sunday morning in time for the service.

That delivery was my assignment, an errand I performed sullenly, unwillingly, and resentfully, fearful of gusts of wind, squalls of rain, a hole in the street, a reckless driver in another car blithely unaware that a sudden stop could inundate and strangle me in a blizzard of sugar, nuts, parsley, sweet white seedless currants, and silver dragées.

To reduce the chances of such a calamity, my wife rode beside me, the tray of Koliva balanced carefully across her knees. When we had a second tray, she rode in the back seat, one tray on her knees while holding the rim of the second tray on the seat beside her. A third tray required us to make two trips until my son was old enough to join us. While driving the burdened mile from our house to the church, I evangelized zealously to my family on the sins of false pride.

When we parked before the church, I carried the trays, one at a time, up the stone steps. Other families arriving to attend church walked up the steps around me. Even as they greeted me pleasantly I envisioned mockery and laughter dragooning me from their eyes because my mother made and I delivered Koliva for the dead. Our occupation made of my family a cabal of vultures, a covey of ghouls. And I

179

marveled that in all the journals and notebooks of writers I had read, none of them ever mentioned Koliva, which made the bloody wheat a rare and dreadful disease that belonged to me alone.

Through those years I came to hate the goddam trays of Koliva with a virulent passion. I despised every detail of the preparation. The boiling kettles filling the house with rank steam as if from a witches' cauldron. The tables spread with the drying wheat. The mute, resigned labor of my wife on Sunday morning. Finally, the humiliating delivery of the trays to the church where my father had served with honor as the priest, where our family was known to everyone.

Sometimes, in a petulant revolt, I refused to deliver the trays. Then my mother engaged in a frantic last-minute effort to find other means of delivery. She phoned customers that I had taken sick, that my car had broken down, and asked them to pick up the trays themselves. The lies and the confusion, added to the complaints of customers whose clothing had been sprayed by sugar, were painful enough so that the following Sunday I returned, like Sisyphus, to the eternal task.

I tried many times to console myself that my wife and mother had the worst of it, that their labor was much more stringent and demanding than the brief time required for delivery. There was even a beneficial lesson in humility, I told my pride, if I only had the courage to absorb it. But all my rationalizations fled as I hurried with bent head up the steps of the church to deliver the glistening, ornamented trays. I became so desperate that the death of a parishioner I barely knew caused me to mourn as if I were a member of his family. And one dreadful week when three members of the parish died, I was outraged at the lengths people were willing to go to embroider my humiliation.

In between the trays of Koliva I continued working at various jobs, and continued the writing of my stories. I made small, fitful advances. The critiques from editors on my rejected stories grew longer. I was encouraged and advised, but still not published. Over a two-year period I began, suffered with, and completed a novel. That bulky appendage joined my stories in the mail at a considerable increase in the cost of postage.

Publishing-house editors wrote me brief memos praising the novel's power, but clearly dismayed by the excesses, the lurid language and incident, the lack of discipline and control. I revenged myself by writing notes back to them, questioning their ability to distinguish poetry from prunes, suggesting they become plumbers in a colony of leeches. Fortunately, I retained enough reason so that I never mailed any of these letters. Finally, two editors whose opinions I valued and whose criticism I respected, Nancy Reynolds of the Atlantic Monthly Press and Dudley Strassberg of World Publishing Company, wrote me long, detailed letters defining with relentless clarity the glaring faults of the novel, advising me against any effort to salvage the book, because the story was simply not worth it. Even as I unhappily accepted that what they wrote me must be true, I felt like a father with a deformed child, advised by well-meaning friends to strangle the baby and try again. In the end I put the book away forever, and consoled myself that I may have learned something about writing from the discarded 75,000 words.

On several occasions, wearying of the endless frustration, the ironic queries, "Are you *still* writing?" "You haven't sold anything *yet?*" I resolved to quit. I managed to maintain my decision for a couple of weeks, but the emptiness of my days gouged me more harshly than the disappointment of the rejections. I always began writing again, determined to make a fresh beginning, planning to destroy work I had done before that time. On one such night I entered our kitchen with a dozen stories in my hands and announced melodramatically to my wife and mother that I was going into the basement to burn them. Relishing my wife's distraught pleas for me to reconsider my awesome decision, I stamped down to the basement and flung open the furnace door. At the first terrible glimpse of the roaring fire, my resolve howled cravenly and fled. I quickly closed the furnace door. Then, unable to muster the courage to walk back through the kitchen clutching the unburned stinkpots of my prose, I hid the manuscripts in the basement to retrieve them after everyone else was asleep. Before my wife and mother I played the role of a strong and determined surgeon who had just amputated his own gangrenous right arm.

I do not believe that one story is suddenly good enough to publish and all the stories that preceded that one, worthless. More likely there is a gradual evolvement, a slow improvement, an absorbing and digesting of small skills learned through the process of writing.

I had gradually been turning away from the contrived sagas of pimps, whores, gunmen, and thieves, from the bloody and clumsy parodies of Greek tragedies. Little by little I had moved back into the experiences I was familiar with, the experiences growing up in my father's parish, the Greek immigrants tenuously suspended between the harshness of the acerbic city and the verdant memory of the land they had left behind them.

Slowly, painfully, and reluctantly, I think I had begun to understand and to accept that writing had to be approached as a profession. One does not expect to practice medicine, law, or architecture without years of study. Why should anyone suppose that the art of writing well can be achieved through some capsulized and abridged route? Mastering a blueprint, arguing a case in law, performing a delicate operation, might even be less of a herculean task than encompassing the schemata of pleasure and folly, misfortune and love, vice and elegance, perfidy, betrayal, vengeance, devotion. It is an undertaking as hazardous as seeking to capture the old man of the sea, the mythical Proteus who constantly eludes the grasp and forever changes shape and form.

For if the riddle of the player's art is how a man can so project himself into a play that he weeps for the anguish of the king, there is a greater mystery in how a writer reshapes into stories the dreams, joys, and terrors that have shaped him. As he works building this strange and haunting life within his life, the panic, fury, and desperation are driven out of him. Finally, he writes, as I began to write, with a curious calmness and resignation, no longer hopeful of anything, but content in those rare, matchless hours when my heart seemed a honeycomb of joy.

One of the last stories of this calmer period was one titled *Pericles on 31st Street*. The story told of an old Greek vendor with a pushcart of hot dogs and peanuts, a defiant old man burning with pride in his heritage who teaches that pride to a group of storekeepers exploited by a landlord they were fearful of challenging.

In the early fall of 1956 I sent *Pericles* to *The Atlantic Monthly.* I had become, I thought, inured to the weeks and often months required for an answer. But as time went on I could not avoid inflating my hopes. I did so in spite of having learned from bitter experience that someone in the editorial department could be on vacation, an editor recalled into the Navy, or, the hardest blow of all, a manuscript had been lost.

I was selling real estate in Hyde Park that year, an occupation that allowed me greater freedom of movement but no more income than I was accustomed to earning. As the weeks passed after the submission of the story to *The Atlantic* and I received no answer, I could not prevent an occasional twinge of expectation, a sudden surge of hope I believed I had given up. By the end of the second month without an answer, I began bagging the days like peaches, taking a small, sweet bite from each one.

On the 17th of December, with the prospect of a bleak and lean Christmas before us, three months after I had submitted *Pericles,* I wired Edward Weeks. I apologized for my impatience and pleaded with him to put my anxiety to rest. Were they seriously considering my story?

His answer arrived the following day, a telegram delivered to me at the real estate office, a telegram I could hardly open because my hands were shaking so violently:

YES. WITH SOME CUTS WE BELIEVE YOUR PERICLES WILL QUALIFY AS A VERY AMUSING ATLANTIC FIRST. CONGRATULATIONS AND MERRY CHRISTMAS. EDWARD WEEKS

There are events like volcanic eruptions in the common filament of our months and our years, upheavals that leave us forever changed. Often they are clock-setting moments having to do with life and death. The radiance of my wife's face as she held our first son in her arms in the hospital bed. The ageless face of my father, moments after he died. And that instant in the real estate office holding the telegram notifying me that I had sold a story after almost ten years of writing and submitting stories remains an unmatched memory I will remember as long as I live.

I drove home to show the telegram to my wife and mother. My wife laughed and cried as she read the telegram over and over, sometimes aloud, sometimes to herself. My mother embraced me, told me to pray in thanks to God. My young sons, confused and a little frightened in the beginning at our shouts and cries, soon laughed at our laughter.

While my wife began the jubilant phoning of relatives and friends, calling my sister in Kansas and my brother in California, I started back for work. On the way I parked before the Rockefeller Chapel on the University of Chicago campus and walked into the silent and shadowed cathedral. I sat down in a pew near the back of the church.

I had struggled long enough to know that the sale of one story was only a beginning, that I would have to write harder than before, that for a long time I would not be spared the trays of Koliva.

But nothing could spoil that moment. I sat there alone and cried wild and grateful tears for the redeeming of my life, for, like Lazarus, the miracle of being reborn once again.